GROWING MUSHROOMS
for beginners

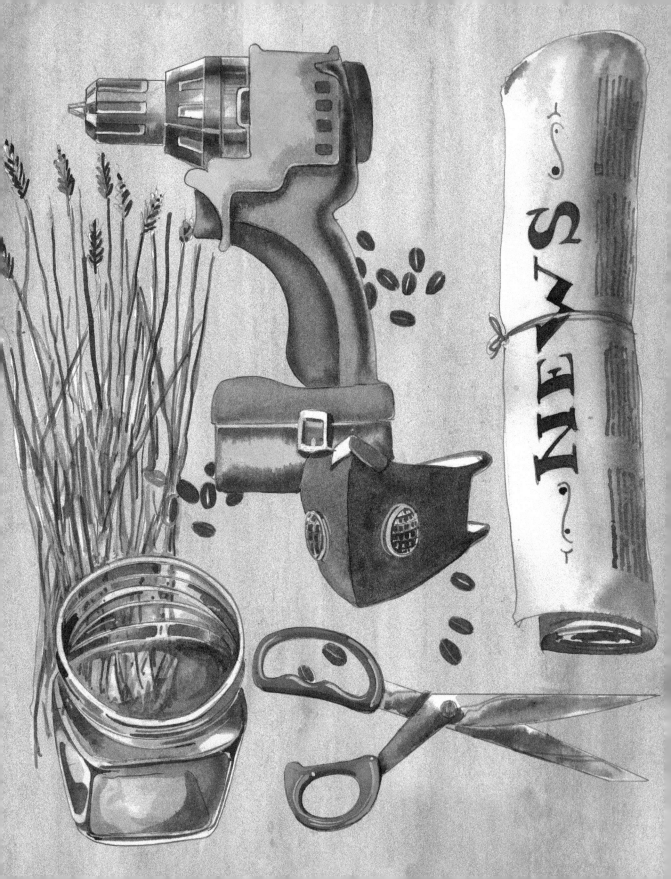

GROWING MUSHROOMS
for beginners

A SIMPLE GUIDE TO CULTIVATING MUSHROOMS AT HOME

SARAH DALZIEL-KIRCHHEVEL ✐ ILLUSTRATIONS BY LIAM O'FARRELL

ROCKRIDGE
PRESS

For general information on our other products
and services or to obtain technical support, please
contact our Customer Care Department within
the United States at (866) 744-2665, or outside the
United States at (510) 253-0500.

Rockridge Press publishes its books in a variety of
electronic and print formats. Some content that
appears in print may not be available in electronic
books, and vice versa.

Interior and Cover Designer: Monica Cheng
Art Producer: Hannah Dickerson
Associate Editor: Maxine Marshall
Production Manager: Martin Worthington
Production Editor: Melissa Edeburn

Illustrations © 2021 Liam O'Farrell
Author photo courtesy of Chris Dalziel,
Joybilee Farm

ISBN: Print 978-1-64876-812-5
eBook 978-1-64876-238-3

R0

To my parents and husband,
who were always supportive and
encouraging while I was writing,
and to my daughter,
who made her appearance
in the middle of working on this book.

TABLE OF CONTENTS

INTRODUCTION

Mushrooms are unique in the plant kingdom. They have mycelium, not roots, and spores, not seeds. They spring out of nowhere, on lawns and in the forest, and disappear when the ground dries. My fascination with mushrooms began early on. As a child I was homeschooled, and I learned how to make spore prints to identify wild mushrooms and determine whether they were safe to eat. Not long afterward, we purchased an oyster mushroom grow-kit. Over the course of just a few days, I watched the mushrooms pin (the very first sign of mushroom growth). Even as a child, I enjoyed the unique flavor of homegrown mushrooms. Accidentally producing mushrooms in my compost pile was my second foray into mushroom growing and led me to ask myself, "Why not grow them deliberately?"

I continued my mushroom journey by inoculating aspen and alder logs to grow oyster and shiitake mushrooms (a project included in this book). I enjoyed the small yield of these logs—a few pounds of fresh mushrooms each spring and sometimes a little extra with the autumn rains. I discovered that mushroom logs, a short-lived perennial that lasts three to five years, were excellent for the home grower.

If you enjoy fresh mushrooms, you will likely find growing your own to be a worthwhile and fun project. You can set up mushroom substrate in many ways, and being creative with your methods can bring great joy. I've fruited mushrooms in a repurposed salad container, a denim bag, and even a burlap potato sack, all filled with straw, cardboard, coffee grounds, and mushroom spawn.

The projects in this book will guide you in cultivating edible and medicinal mushrooms in your backyard, garden, shed, or spare room, or on your deck. The skill you develop while completing one project will help you with the others. Once you have mastered the processes of preparation, sanitization, and pasteurization, mushroom growing becomes simple.

After cultivating and harvesting your mushrooms, you'll find this book's recipes a delicious way to enjoy them. Nothing beats sharing a dish with friends or family and mentioning that you cultivated its gorgeous mushrooms. If you happen to grow more mushrooms than you can use, this book will guide you through the basics of freezing or drying them.

I'm sure you will find growing your own mushrooms to be a rewarding process. Enjoy the fruits of your labor with simple and tasty recipes and effective preservation methods. Experiment and have fun!

Part I

Gardens of Earthy Delights

Historically, mushrooms were enjoyed by peasant and king alike, although the type of mushroom varied. Certain varieties are tied in to the idea of a delicacy, and many of the mushrooms you can grow at home are considered gourmet. Creating your own mushroom garden is a fantastic way to enjoy these tasty, earthy treasures at their prime.

Chapter 1

Step-by-Step Cultivation Guide

Mushrooms are more enigmatic than your normal house and garden plants. One day there's little sign of them; the next, the mushroom pins form, and by evening or a few days later, you have full mushrooms. A bit of background information will help remove the mystery from growing and cultivating your own mushrooms. Growing them is easy, not esoteric, and possible to do even from your living room. Mushrooms can be houseplants; they just look different. And they taste delicious.

Why Grow Your Own?

One reason to grow mushrooms at home is to have fresh gourmet mushrooms ready at your fingertips. Although many stores sell gourmet mushrooms, they are not always available when you want them, and many varieties, like shiitake, are available dried more often than fresh. When you grow your own, you can try varieties that are less commercially viable because they are fragile or difficult to transport.

The mushrooms you grow yourself are fresher, at peak tastiness, and less expensive than commercially grown mushrooms. You'll also know that the mushrooms are safe from potential chemical exposure.

If you produce more mushrooms than you can eat fresh, you can safely dry or freeze them. We've all bought mushrooms thinking we'll use them right away, only to compost many of them later. Growing your own can cut down on that kind of food waste.

All the mushrooms included in this book are great for culinary use and have additional health and wellness benefits. They provide fiber and protein, can help enhance immune function, and contain antioxidants. Mushrooms that have been exposed to direct sunlight are also packed with vitamin D. Drying homegrown mushrooms at the peak of freshness to grind and use in adaptogenic hot cocoa blends, or to freeze and add to stir-fries and other foods, is a great way to invest in your health and wellness.

Working within your space and time constraints, you'll find that even a small mushroom log or colonized substrate can produce an abundance.

Cultivation at a Glance

As you will discover through the projects in this book, mushroom cultivation is simple. Here's an overview of that process.

1. **Pick a mushroom.** Read the profiles in the "Meet the Mushrooms" section (pages 5 to 19) to choose the right mushroom for your circumstances. Some mushrooms, like shiitakes, grow well only on hardwoods, whereas others, like oyster mushrooms, will colonize on many mediums, including cardboard.

2. **Dampen the substrate (growing medium) and form.** Some mushrooms prefer a wood medium; others will colonize on coffee grounds, straw, paper, and other materials.

3. **Inoculate the substrate with spawn (spores from your chosen mushroom).** You can purchase spawned forms such as sawdust, plugs (pieces of dowel mycelated with a desired mushroom type), and grain. You can even start mushrooms from other mushrooms.

4. **Colonize.** Sit tight until the white mycelium becomes a thick, colonized mat.

5. **Grow and harvest.** Water or mist the mycelium to encourage growth. Pins form at gas exchange points. When the mushrooms have reached their full size, cut or twist them off.

❧ A LITTLE MYCOLOGY ❧

Mushrooms belong to the fungi kingdom. Mushroom mycelium grows throughout a substrate, breaking down that material to gain the energy it needs to grow. When that food source is depleted, the mushroom sends up pins to form fruiting heads that release spores, which the wind spreads to other substrates, perpetuating the mushroom's lifecycle.

Saprobic mushrooms, the kind that break down organic matter to make energy, are the focus of this book. They grow large caps and fruit off non-living material such as fallen logs, sawdust and wood chips, straw, grains, and even paper products made from wood cellulose. Saprobic mushrooms thrive by enzymatically breaking down the cellulose in these materials to release the other basic molecules they need to grow. They fruit once conditions are ideal for spores to survive. That fruit is the mushroom we consume.

Meet the Mushrooms

Most of the mushrooms described in this section can easily be cultivated by beginning growers, and they are commonly featured in recipes and restaurant dishes, used in health products, and available in food stores. When choosing which mushrooms to grow, you'll want to consider not only your taste preferences, but also your space and time constraints.

Although the mushrooms highlighted here can be grown both indoors and outdoors, some are better off in a particular environment. Wine caps, for example, thrive in outdoor garden conditions, whereas oyster species work great for experimental and small-scale indoor growing because they can colonize nearly any medium.

Agaricus (*Agaricus bisporus*)

Aliases: Cremini, Portabella, White Button

Characteristics: young mushroom gills are pink in appearance, whereas older mushrooms develop a darker brown gill; tops can be white or brown, depending on the age and the timing of the flush (referring to the crop or group of mushrooms that appears around the same time period, but can also mean "fruiting body")

Beginner Friendliness: easy-to-moderate; spawn is easy to source; requires slightly higher fruiting temperature than other varieties; can be picky about substrate; colonizes slowly; mycelium transfer among substrate types is difficult

Flavors: mild, classic mushroom taste; absorbs flavors from other ingredients

Health Benefits: provides fiber and protein; supports the immune system and helps regulate blood pressure and blood sugar levels; is an excellent source of copper, phosphorus, potassium, selenium, vitamin B complex, vitamin D, and zinc

Cooking: Agaricus mushrooms are considered suitable for any culinary use. They work well sautéed, in sauces, or as a topping on steak or pizza. They stand up well in noodle dishes, soups, and stir-fries.

Time Commitment: 2 to 4 hours for initial colonization and sterilization; 5 minutes a day to check on colonization and to ensure other fungi do not outcompete them; mycelation usually complete in 1 month with first flush appearing in 6 to 8 weeks

Inoculation: Spawn for agaricus mushrooms is normally available as grain or sawdust, although sawdust can be slow to transfer to the desired fruiting substrate unless supplemented with bran or grain.

Colonization: In a pure culture, the mycelium of agaricus mushrooms appears cottony but develops a warted appearance as it grows and forms microbial partnerships. Until they fully colonize, agaricus mushrooms require monitoring of substrate for mold growth.

Harvesting: To harvest these mushrooms, pull them out of the ground by hand, trim the stem butts, and wash. Replant the stem butts in a new substrate, if desired, or compost the trimmings. Alternatively, use a knife to cut the mushrooms off at ground level. Agaricus mushrooms can be refrigerated for up to 2 weeks.

Cordyceps (*Cordyceps militaris*)

Aliases: none

Characteristics: thin fruiting bodies; more like fingers than mushrooms

Beginner Friendliness: somewhat difficult for beginners because of slow growth rate; spawn can be hard to source and slow to start

Flavors: sweet; similar to chicken broth

Health Benefits: warms and energizes; strengthens; reduces inflammation and stress; boosts immunity

Cooking: These mushrooms are generally consumed in extracts and powders for health benefits rather than for culinary purposes, unless used in a broth. Because cordyceps mushrooms are woody (tough) when they are fresh, they are best used dried.

Time Commitment: 6 hours for inoculation setup; 15 to 30 minutes a day for monitoring; several months for fruiting

Inoculation: Cordyceps mushrooms spawn must be prepared in a sterile environment. They grow best on combination spawn, usually agar and grain. Ask for spawn recommendations from your supplier because varieties from different sources and countries of origin may have specific grain preferences. If possible, source spawn in syringes.

Colonization: Cordyceps mushrooms are slow-growing colonizers and are best grown in small quantities or small containers. Adjust the food with each regrowth or new batch, and don't divide the mycelated substrate too frequently.

Harvesting: Cut or pull off cordyceps fingers as they develop the orange or powdery dust of the perithecium, this mushroom type's spore sacs. The fingers can be longer than your container and form interesting shapes. Fruiting can begin up to 2 weeks before harvest time. Use fresh mushrooms in broth, or immediately dehydrate your harvest.

Lion's Mane (*Hericium erinaceus*)

Aliases: Hedgehog Mushroom, Pom Pom

Characteristics: fuzzy or spiny appearance; fresh, young mushrooms are white; color tone changes to brownish-orange as the mushrooms age

Beginner Friendliness: medium difficulty for both outdoor and indoor growing; slow growing; may not be a good choice for first-time growers

Flavors: crab- or lobster-like taste

Health Benefits: higher protein content than most other mushrooms; high level of antioxidant properties; contains iron and potassium

Cooking: Shred lion's mane mushrooms and sauté the strips in butter with lemon and garlic to enhance their lobster-like flavor. These mushrooms go well with seafood and vegetables. Although they freeze well, they do not reconstitute well from dried form but can be used as a dry powder. They are classified as medicinal.

Time Commitment: 2 days for setup; 2 hours for initial inoculation; 5 minutes a day for monitoring colonization progress; 4 to 6 weeks from inoculation to first flush but up to 10 months from inoculation to harvest, if starting from seed spawn or plugs (hardwood dowels inoculated with mycelium spawn)

Inoculation: Look for sawdust, plug, or cardboard spawns for lion's mane mushrooms. A kit may be available.

Colonization: The mycelium of lion's mane mushrooms is fragile. These mushrooms do not typically outcompete other species. They fruit best on hardwood logs or sawdust blocks. You can expect only one flush per year from logs or bags with only one mushroom developing at a time. Plan to keep small colonized blocks for at least two years. The mycelium may prefer coolish temperatures.

Harvesting: Harvest the mushroom just as spines start to form, cutting it off close to the log but leaving a small amount of flesh attached. Doing so will enable a secondary mushroom to form, so you can get more than one mushroom, per log, per flush.

Oyster (*Pleurotus sp.*)

Aliases: Blue, Florida, Golden, King Oyster, Pearl, Phoenix, Pink

Characteristics: grows in clusters; long gills extend from the edge of the cap to the stem

Beginner Friendliness: exceptional; aggressive colonizer; will outcompete most other fungi and molds; standard mushroom for all-in-one grow-kits

Flavors: nutty; hints of fruity and meaty tones

Health Benefits: strong B vitamin profile with folate, niacin, pantothenic acid, riboflavin, thiamin, and vitamin B6; trace minerals include copper, iron, magnesium, manganese, phosphorus, potassium, selenium, and zinc

Cooking: Oyster mushrooms are delicious when lightly sautéed with butter. They pair well with fish, meats, seafood, and vegetables, and they will work in any recipe that calls for mushrooms. Although they can be dried, oyster mushrooms should be powdered rather than rehydrated.

Time Commitment: 1 hour for inoculation; 1 to 2 minutes a day for a few weeks to monitor mycelium growth, moisture, and harvest timing

Inoculation: Oyster mushrooms will grow well on home-sterilized substrates, especially wood-cellulose or blended substrates.

Colonization: Mycelium colonize rapidly and can be ready for fruiting in just a few weeks. Golden oysters have the widest fruiting temperature and therefore are more suitable for cool environments.

Harvesting: Harvest the mushroom clusters by twisting free the entire cluster at its base. Fresh oyster mushrooms will keep up to 2 weeks in a paper bag in the refrigerator.

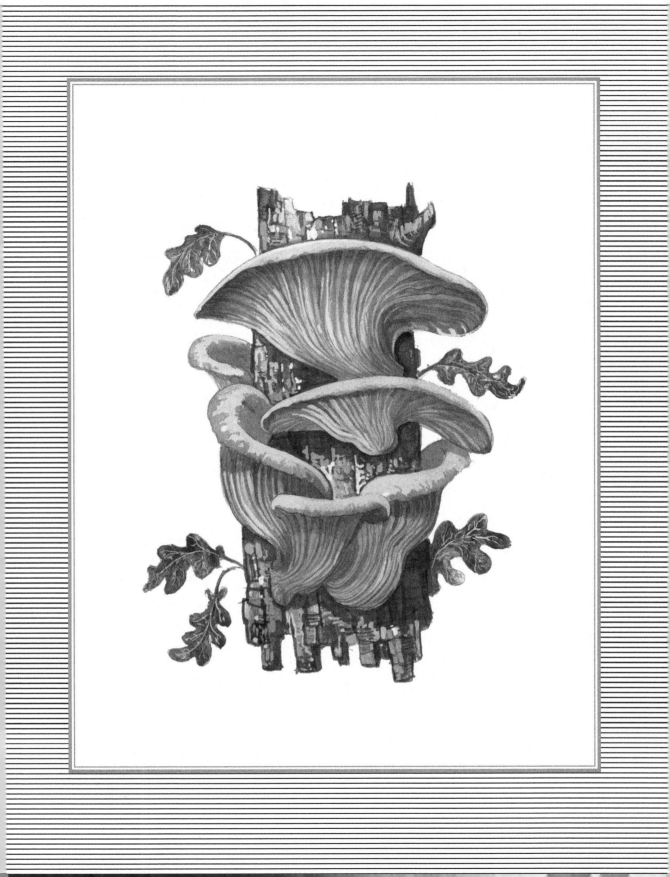

Reishi (*Ganoderma sp.*)

Aliases: Artist Conk, Hemlock Reishi, Ling Chi

Characteristics: rough fan shape; bright orange-brown banding; fruiting bodies begin as an antler (long hornlike form), then fan out into the classic fan (conk)

Beginner Friendliness: fairly easy for indoor and outdoor cultivation

Flavors: strong meaty tones; used most frequently in broths or soups

Health Benefits: high beta-glucan levels provide immune support; cardiovascular and digestive properties include regulating blood pressure and lowering cholesterol; anti-bacterial, anti-inflammatory, and anti-viral traits

Cooking: In powdered form or as extracts, reishi mushrooms are used for flavor and health benefits in broths and soups. They are tough and normally not consumed fresh.

Time Commitment: few hours for inoculation; few minutes a day for monitoring; up to 10 or more months of growth from inoculation to fruiting on outdoor logs

Inoculation: These mushrooms dislike being exposed to air and light. Inoculated logs should be shallowly buried after the first few weeks of colonizing. Indoors, the mushrooms should be grown in sealed plastic with minimal light and air exchange. Hemlock reishi is the only reishi that will grow on conifer logs; all other mushrooms of this species require hardwood.

Colonization: When fully colonized, the reishi mycelium is one of the strongest of all the mushroom mycelia. To encourage fruiting, leave the grow-bag sealed and ensure adequate space at the top of the bag for antlers to develop.

Harvesting: Harvest several weeks after antlers develop. Cut the antlers off the mycelium block with a sharp knife. Immediately slice and dry them for storage, or use them fresh in soups, broths, teas, or alcohol infusions.

Shiitake (*Lentinula edodes*)

Aliases: Black Forest, Chinese Black, Oakwood

Characteristics: light brown stem; dark brown umbrella-shaped cap; white hairs on the surface

Beginner Friendliness: very; growth spring to autumn on sawdust or logs

Flavors: meaty or yeasty; chewy texture

Health Benefits: excellent source of copper and selenium; contain a combination of B vitamins (B3, B6, folate, and choline), fiber, manganese, vitamin D, and zinc

Cooking: Shiitakes are traditionally added to miso soup. Try them in hearty sauces or serve them on their own as a side dish for beef, chicken, lamb, tofu, or venison. To give your vegetable stock extra depth, add dried shiitake mushrooms or just the stems.

Time Commitment: a few days for preparing and inoculating logs; a few hours for inoculating sawdust; 5 minutes every few days for maintenance, unless coaxing a flush by soaking or otherwise shocking a block of mycelium or a mycelated log; mycelation complete in about a month with fruiting in about 2 to 3 months

Inoculation: Shiitakes prefer 70 to 80°F. They work especially well when grown in sawdust or on alder, birch, cherry, sugar maple, and white oak. Logs should be cut in autumn and stored off the ground.

Colonization: Logs are fully colonized when white-to-brown mycelium appears on their ends; fruiting will occur after this point. In sawdust, mycelium browns with age. A slightly warty surface the size of cotton balls will begin to be visible 3 weeks from the start of the project. When all the sawdust is colonized, cut holes in the plastic to permit the mushrooms to begin forming pins.

Harvesting: Harvest shiitakes when the caps are open and 2 to 3 inches wide. They should be firm to the touch at the base but have a little bounce when the cap is pressed with a finger. With a sharp knife, cut the mushrooms off close to the log.

Wine Cap (*Stropharia rugoso-annulata*)

Aliases: Garden Giant, King Stropharia

Characteristics: red caps and white stems when young; burgundy gills and brownish-red caps when mature

Beginner Friendliness: easy to grow outdoors; slightly more difficult to grow indoors

Flavors: cashew and herb notes; sometimes described as tasting like potatoes cooked in wine

Health Benefits: small amounts of fiber, vitamin D, amino acids, protein, iron, and copper; trace amounts of calcium; may have mild anticoagulant properties

Cooking: Wine caps complement nutty and herbal flavors. Use them in stir-fries and wine sauces and as accompaniments for eggs, fish, poultry, tofu, and vegetables. Do not consume them for more than 3 consecutive days. They can cause gastric upset if eaten too frequently. Wine caps are not as shelf-stable as some of the other mushrooms, but their caps dry and rehydrate well.

Time Commitment: 2 to 3 hours for indoor setup; less than 1 hour for outdoor or garden setup; 5 to 10 minutes every few days for maintenance and harvesting; mycelation about 2 weeks to 1 month with a harvest at 6 weeks to 2 months

Inoculation: Wine caps prefer sawdust spawn or a mixture of sawdust and compost. They can be started from a few threads of mycelium in damp, refrigerated cardboard. They are an aggressive colonizer and are beneficial for outdoor gardens because they consume harmful soil nematodes (small worms).

Colonization: Wine caps grow most aggressively outdoors but can also give rise to large flushes indoors. Comparatively large, these mushrooms will outcompete other fungi. For indoor growing, fruit these mushrooms in a grain or a combined grain and sawdust substrate. Wine caps will grow in compost piles.

Harvesting: Harvest these mushrooms before their caps fully open and while the veil is still attached. They have the best flavor when they are immature. Pull them from the base so some mycelium remains attached. Replant the loose mycelium in a garden or along a pathway.

Dedicate Space

You don't need much more space for growing mushrooms than you do for a regular houseplant. My first experiment was on a shelf in an open closet; my second sat on top of a bookcase. Just be sure to keep them away from any drying heat sources, such as a radiator or woodstove. An open shelf in a spare room or a corner of a kitchen counter in a small apartment should work equally well.

Growing mushrooms on logs can require a bit more space than for other substrates, but doesn't have to. The size of the log will determine the need. A shaded balcony or deck may work for storing the project while waiting for the mycelium to colonize the log. Keep mushrooms out of direct sun to avoid drying them out. If you live in a dry climate, the logs will need watering. A misting system can help keep mushroom logs happy.

Some people choose to use modified plastic tents and grow-lights for their developing mushrooms. Those with yards and gardens can inoculate wood-chip paths to encourage mushrooms to grow naturally outdoors.

Pick a Medium

Each mushroom type has a substrate preference. Logs look great and don't need to be sterilized, but they can be bulky or difficult to find. Sawdust and wood chips are easy to find and can be conveniently packed into containers. The same goes for cellulose-based mediums like cardboard, coffee grounds, newspaper, straw, or whole grains, all of which are easy to sterilize and fit into your container of choice.

When first starting out, choose your substrate based on your available space. A firewood-size log may be a great choice for open growing on a kitchen counter and will be decorative during fruiting. Or, you may want to pack sawdust, or another fine-grained medium, in a plastic bag that you keep sealed and move around at will until it's time to encourage fruiting. I've grown mushrooms in recycled plastic salad containers, a heavy plastic bag, and a recycled cloth bag. The key to simplicity is keeping the substrate contained, damp, and easily moved.

❧ ALL-IN-ONE KITS ❧

If you're nervous about taking the plunge into growing your own mushrooms or are afraid your mushrooms will be outcompeted by common molds, consider a grow-kit. Choose from several mushroom types, though the most common is the oyster. Usually, a grow-kit is a solidly mycelated block of compact sawdust shipped in a heavy plastic bag. Once you're ready, cut a few holes in the bag, mist the substrate, and maintain the contents according to the kit's instructions to see the magic of mushrooms fruiting in your own kitchen.

Most all-in-one mushroom kits provide a low-risk introduction. They will give you two flushes of mushrooms, possibly three, and because you won't need to inoculate a substrate, your focus will be solely on mushroom care—balancing humidity levels, providing the amount of warmth mushrooms like, and monitoring the fruiting process. Kits typically cost anywhere from $25 to $40.

Source Spawn Cultures

To begin your mushroom-growing experiments, you may be tempted to go out and buy a mushroom. Pre-inoculated spawn is a lot easier because you don't need a sterile space and you're guaranteed a strong and active mushroom strain. If you do want to try to start mushrooms from mushrooms, however, we will cover some of the steps and techniques in chapter 6 (see page 77). For now, sourcing spawn from a reputable supplier will be the easiest method of starting.

Spawn types depend on the mushroom type and its feeding preferences. Most spawn suppliers will have sawdust or grain spawn available. Spawn sold in plugs or syringes are more expensive options. No matter who you order from, you should be able to specify the spawn and mushroom types to make sure you get one that will thrive and fruit in your temperatures.

Grain, Sawdust, and Straw

Grain, sawdust, and straw spawns are sterile mediums used to inoculate a sterile medium to grow mushrooms. These spawns are best used for inoculating loose, sterile material packed into spawning bags or containers.

Many commercial growers provide large heavy-duty plastic bags packed with sterile substrate mixed with one of these three spawn types. These spawn types can be used to inoculate small bags or boxes of substrate for home growing or be used to introduce mushrooms to outdoor gardens.

Plugs

Most mushroom spawn suppliers offer plug spawn, in addition to other types. A plug spawn is a hardwood dowel inoculated with mushrooms and is specific for working with logs. Plug spawn is most often used with tree-loving lion's mane, oyster, reishi, and shiitake mushrooms.

Plugs are the easiest spawn type to use with logs. All you need to do is create correctly sized holes in the log, place a plug in each hole, and seal. Inoculating logs using the cheaper sawdust spawn adds more steps, tools, and effort, but can be done.

Spore Syringes

Spore syringes, as the name suggests, are syringes filled with nutrient mix and mushroom spore or mycelium. Inoculating with a spore syringe makes maintaining sterility easy and efficient without the need for lab equipment and is the best method for slow-growing mushroom types. For example, cordyceps may be best procured using a spore or mycelium syringe because of their slow rate of growing and a general lack of availability of cordyceps spore or spawned mycelium in other forms.

Syringes can also be used to inoculate grow bags, or for growing out mycelium before starting a grow bag. Syringes are not recommended with hardwood logs because the spawn may not end up deep enough in the wood.

THE MUSHROOM GROWER'S
❧ GLOSSARY ❦

Flush: a crop of mushrooms; also used to refer to the fruiting body of a mushroom

Growing medium: substrate; the organic material mushrooms will grow on; potting soil is to plants what growing medium is to mushrooms

Gypsum: hydrated calcium sulfate used as a nutritive additive for mushroom growing; can be found in fertilizer sections of gardening stores

Hand of mushrooms: specific to the clustered growth pattern or "hands" of oyster mushrooms, as opposed to the growth of individual mushrooms, such as with shiitake

Inoculate: the act of seeding mushrooms into new substrate, either with spawn or spores, with the intention of letting them grow

Mycelated: the growth of mushroom mycelium throughout a portion of substrate

Mycelium: the mushroom equivalent of roots; can resemble mold

Nematode: a type of soil parasite that attacks plant roots and can destroy gardens

Pasteurization: the process of bringing material to a temperature of 130°F and maintaining it for at least 30 minutes to remove pathogens and unwanted bacteria or fungus

Pinning: the earliest aboveground part of the mushroom; this stage takes place before the "pin" swells to a full "cap" during the fruiting stage

Reemay: also known as a floating row cover; a type of light fabric used in gardening to protect plants from frost and insect damage

Spawn: substrate that has mushrooms growing in it already, which is used to seed mushrooms in a new substrate

Substrate: pasteurized or sterilized growing medium that is ready to have mushrooms start growing in it, or that has mushrooms growing on it already

Chapter 2

Growing on a Log

Logs are the most common medium for mushroom growing and can yield visually spectacular results. Almost all the mushrooms profiled in this book will grow well on different types of hardwood logs. To start, check the wood type preference of your desired mushrooms. Order the log and a plug or sawdust spawn, then get some wax (any candle is fine). Now you are ready to grow delicious mushrooms.

The Basics

Lion's mane, oyster species, reishi, and shiitake prefer log-based substrates over sawdust or compost mediums. Fully colonizing a log with mycelium can take one to six months, depending on the size of the log and type of mushroom. A 16- to 18-inch-long log, 5 to 8 inches in diameter, can be fully colonized in one or two months. For apartment growing, this smaller size is great. For outdoor growing, 4-foot-long logs, about 5 inches in diameter, are usually recommended.

Talk to someone who sources firewood to get green log rounds, or a tree removal service to see if they'll give you logs or heavy branches. Aim for aspen, beech, birch, maple, or oak for the wood-loving mushrooms in this book. Don't use treated lumber and aim for logs harvested in autumn or winter, before the spring sap run. Doing so helps the bark remain firmly attached to the wood beneath and prolongs the life of the mushroom log by a year or two. With the right conditions, most mushroom logs can fruit for three to five years. While waiting for colonization and fruiting, keep your log shaded and off the ground to prevent drying and to help mushrooms thrive.

Water the logs about every week if the environment is not too dry (more often if you live somewhere arid) and you are not trying to coax a flush. When you are trying to coax a flush, however, soak the log with water and, again, keep it in a shaded area. Most logs will naturally produce both a spring and autumn flush of mushrooms, if outdoors. Keep in mind that coaxing flushes beyond two will shorten the lifespan of the log.

King Oyster Mushroom Cultivation

King oyster mushrooms are the largest of the oyster mushroom family. As such, they work exceptionally well for growing on logs and, when fruiting, are visually attractive. Oyster mushrooms are among the quickest colonizing mushrooms, with results in just a few months. A small log will take a month to six weeks, from inoculation to full colonizing, and can be coaxed to fruit a few weeks after that.

What You'll Need

A recently cut log of any of these species: American beech, ash, aspen, elm, oak, poplar, red maple, sugar maple, white birch, or willow. Make sure the log has not been treated with any heavy metal or other preservatives. A log cut in the autumn will work best and will retain its bark longest.

King oyster mushroom spawn in sawdust or plug form; source from a reputable supplier when possible.

A drill with a drill bit, if using plug spawn. Be sure the drill bit is the same diameter as the plugs, which can vary in size, although ⅛ inch is common.

A sawdust plug tool, if using sawdust spawn

Wax for sealing the plug holes in the log; beeswax, paraffin, or a soy-based wax are good choices.

A heat source and applicator tool for the wax

A safe and clear space to work

A shaded, slightly damp area to store the mushroom log; protect the surfaces in this area to be able to freely mist and water the log without worrying about water damage.

A flat-ish plastic bowl or container, if you are working indoors, where you will rest your log. Keep your log container cool and exposed to light.

Prepare the Medium

Keep a log you cut yourself off the ground and let it age for at least one month to allow the naturally antifungal properties of the wood to decay. Keeping the log off the ground also prevents wild fungi from starting to colonize before you can introduce your spawn of choice to the log.

For a log you purchase, ask the supplier when the log was felled (if known), and store it off the ground as well. Pre-split firewood with the wood grain exposed will not work well because without bark it will dry out too quickly for the mycelium to proliferate and it will decay faster than logs with bark.

Inoculate

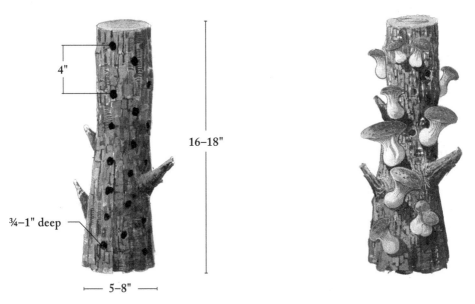

4"

16–18"

¾–1" deep

5–8"

1. Wipe down and sanitize your workspace. I find it most comfortable to work at a waist-high table when possible.

2. If you're using sawdust spawn, sanitize your drill bit and sawdust applicator.

3. Warm up your heat source and melt your sealing wax. Make sure your wax applicator (such as a lit candle or wax batik applicator) is also warmed.

4. Place the log on the table and mark out dots 4 inches apart in a diamond-shaped grid pattern.

5. For plugs ½ inch long, drill a ¾-inch-deep hole at each of the marked dots; for sawdust, drill the hole 1 inch deep.

6. Place a plug or sawdust spawn in the first hole.

7. Seal the hole with melted wax.

8. Repeat steps 6 and 7 for all the holes in the log.

9. Set the log aside, and mist gently. Or if you are growing outdoors, you can inoculate the log the day before a heavy rain to eliminate the need to water or mist the log afterward.

Colonize

1. After inoculating, let the log rest for four to six weeks, watering or misting at least once a week.

2. Flip the log every week, placing the bottom end at top and the top end at bottom to prevent the lower and damper end of the log from colonizing faster than the drier top end.

3. The log is fully colonized when white mycelium starts appearing on both ends. Mycelium can look like mold, but if you scrape the white area with your fingernail and are able to detect an aroma of fresh, tasty mushrooms, you'll know you've got mushroom mycelium.

4. If you are working with multiple logs, place two non-inoculated spacer logs directly on the ground. Build the inoculated logs, log-cabin style, on top of the logs on the ground, forming an open square shape to help the logs preserve moisture and to keep ground-sourced decay to a minimum.

Harvest

1. The best temperatures for fruiting are between 70 and 80°F. For outdoor mushrooms, aim for a period when temperatures are projected to be within that range.

2. Soak the log for a few hours in a small pool of water, if possible. If you don't have a small wading pool, mist the log and its surrounding area multiple times over the course of a day to increase humidity. If it's an indoor log, soak it in a sink of cool water or a bathtub of cool water for 2 to 3 hours before returning it to the drip tray.

3. Cut three to five 1-inch gashes in the bark or drill holes in the log at 6-inch intervals once the log is fully colonized, if the spawn plugs are even with the surface of the log. Sometimes oyster mushrooms will fruit from the spawn plug points.

4. Don't drill more than four to six holes in a 16-inch-long, 8-inch-diameter log. Otherwise, the mushroom can overfruit and will not develop properly.

continues

5. Monitor the mushroom log. Areas where you have provided fruiting holes should begin to develop pins within 24 to 48 hours of soaking the log.

6. Let the mushrooms grow for 1 to 1½ days. If outside, put a protective fabric like reemay over the logs to prevent flies and beetles from attacking the forming mushrooms.

7. When the oyster mushroom caps open and have fully formed their classic trumpet shape, harvest the hand of mushrooms. Individual mushroom caps should measure between 2 and 3 inches across.

8. Cut off the hand of oyster mushrooms from the log with a sharp knife. You can also harvest by pulling the hand off the log, but I find that the knife gives a cleaner finish.

9. Bring your mushrooms indoors and rinse them.

10. Cook your first harvest of homegrown king oyster mushrooms and enjoy! Oyster mushrooms will stay fresh up to 2 weeks if stored in a paper bag in the refrigerator.

Shiitake Mushroom Log Cultivation

Shiitake mushrooms, which have culinary and medicinal uses, grow best on hardwood logs. This friendly mushroom is great for beginning log growers because it provides good yields and is simple to start and harvest. The mushroom is also very pretty. Shiitakes are delicious for fresh gourmet eating and they also dry well.

What You'll Need

A recently cut log of any of these species: alder, oak, maple, birch, poplar, aspen, or American beech. Make sure the log has not been treated with any preservatives, particularly heavy metal preservatives. An autumn-cut log will work best and retain its bark longest. Alder is the softest of these woods and, as such, is least recommended for long-lasting shiitake mushroom logs.

Shiitake mushroom spawn, in either sawdust or plug form. Source from a reputable supplier when possible.

A drill and drill bit, if using plug spawn. Make sure the drill bit is the same diameter as the plugs, which can vary in size, although ⅛ inch is a common size.

Wax for sealing the plug holes in the log

A sawdust plug tool, if using sawdust spawn

A heat source and applicator tool for the wax

A safe and clear space to work

A shaded, slightly damp area to store the mushroom log. The growing area should be water resistant, so you can mist and water the log to encourage mycelium growth.

A flat-ish plastic bowl or container, if you are working indoors, to hold your log. Keep your log container exposed to light in a cool corner of your home.

Prepare the Medium

If you cut the log yourself, keep it off the ground and let it age for at least one month. Doing so lets the naturally antifungal properties of the wood decay, so they won't impact your mushroom growing. Keeping the log off the ground also prevents wild fungi from starting to colonize the log before you can introduce your spawn of choice.

If you are purchasing a log, ask your supplier when the log was felled (if known), and make sure to store it off the ground. Pre-split firewood will not work well for a mushroom log, as the woodgrain is exposed and a log without bark will dry out too quickly for the mycelium to proliferate. Also, logs without bark will decay faster than logs with bark.

Inoculate

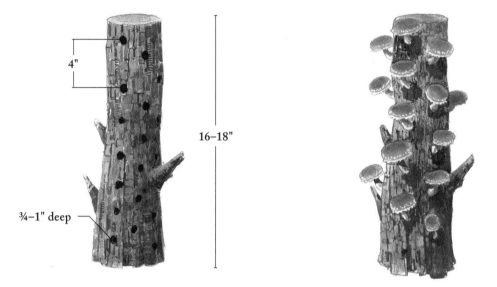

1. Wipe down and sanitize your workspace. I find it most comfortable to work on a waist-height table when possible.

2. If using sawdust spawn, sanitize your drill bit and sawdust applicator.

3. Warm up your heat source and melt your sealing wax. Make sure your wax applicator (such as a lit candle or wax batik applicator) is also warmed up.

4. Place the log on the table and mark out dots 4 inches apart in a diamond-shaped patttern.

5. For plugs ½ inch long, drill a ¾-inch-deep hole on each of the marked dots; for sawdust, drill the hole 1 inch deep.

6. Place a plug or sawdust spawn in the first hole.

7. Seal the hole with melted wax.

8. Repeat steps 6 and 7 for all the holes in the log.

9. Set the log aside, and mist gently. If you are growing outdoors, you can complete these steps the day before a heavy rain is forecast to eliminate the need to water or mist the log after inoculation.

Colonize

1. Shiitake logs will take 8 to 10 months to fully colonize. Colonization can happen faster with smaller logs.

2. If you are doing indoor small log growing, let the log rest for 8 to 10 weeks, watering or misting at least once a week.

3. Flip the log every week, placing the bottom end at top and the top end at bottom to prevent the lower and damper end of the log from colonizing faster than the drier top end.

4. The log is fully colonized when white mycelium starts appearing on both ends. Mycelium can look like mold, but if you scrape the white area with your fingernail and are able to detect an aroma of fresh, tasty mushrooms, you'll know you've got mushroom mycelium.

5. If you are working with multiple logs, place two non-inoculated spacer logs directly on the ground. Build the inoculated logs into an open square shape. Doing so helps the logs preserve moisture and keeps ground-sourced decay to a minimum. Mist or water the logs every week.

Harvest

1. When deciding when to harvest, choose a time frame during which the temperatures are projected to be ideal for your strain. Warm strains need temperatures above 75°F; cool strains like temperatures between 35 and 50°F. For indoor fruiting, keep interior temperature within these ranges.

2. If you would like to force a flush, or encourage a flush to start from indoor growing, start by soaking the log for a few hours in a small pool of water, if possible. If you don't have a small wading pool, mist the log and its surrounding area multiple times over the course of a day to increase the humidity. If it's an indoor log, soak it in a sink of cool water or a bathtub of cool water for 2 to 3 hours before pulling it out and placing it back on its drip tray.

3. Cut a few gashes in the bark if the spawn plugs are even with the surface of the log. Sometimes oyster mushrooms will fruit from the spawn plug points; other times it's best to encourage them by drilling some imitation beetle or woodpecker holes in the log.

4. Don't drill more than four to six holes in a 16-inch-long, 8-inch-diameter log. Otherwise, the mushroom can overfruit and will not be able to develop properly.

5. Monitor the mushroom log. Areas where you have provided fruiting holes should begin to develop pins within 24 to 48 hours of soaking the log.

6. Let the mushrooms grow for 1 to 1½ days. If outside, put protective fabric like reemay over the logs to prevent flies and beetles from attacking the forming mushrooms.

7. When the shiitake mushrooms open, the caps should be light gray or brown with white speckles and measure between 2 and 3 inches in diameter.

8. Cut off shiitake mushrooms from the log with a sharp knife.

9. Bring your mushrooms indoors and rinse them off.

10. Enjoy your first harvest of shiitake mushrooms, which can remain fresh for up to 2 weeks and can be preserved by drying.

❧ TROUBLESHOOTING ❧

My mushrooms formed well but became mushy.

They probably got too much surface water. Once pins form, do not water or mist the mushrooms until you harvest them.

What's growing doesn't look like the species with which I spawned my log.

1. Check other mushroom varieties to try to identify what is growing. Your spawn could have been mislabeled and the mushroom type could still be edible.

2. You may have purchased or procured an already fallen log that was already colonized by wild fungi. If you cannot identify the mushroom type, do not eat it.

3. You may want to keep the log and monitor it to see if your desired fungi fruits later than the wild invader. Or try again with a fresh log and new spawn.

I forgot to flip my indoor log for a few weeks and the bottom is white. It looks like mold.

On your counter, or in a container, mushroom mycelium will remain white and string-like. Lightly scrape this white area, or the bottom of the log itself, and sniff. If you smell mushrooms, you have mycelium. If not, you have mold.

My logs appear fully colonized, but they won't fruit.

Shiitake and oyster mushrooms can take up to a year to fruit on full-size mushroom logs. With smaller indoor logs, try increasing the humidity or ambient light, or adjusting the temperature. Mushrooms that prefer the cool may not fruit as well, or as early, in temperate or warm climates.

My mushrooms are the wrong shape or color. What went wrong?

Mushrooms like diffused light, such as that under a tree canopy. If you store mushroom logs in a closet or cupboard, bring them into diffused daylight for several days before trying to coax a mushroom flush. Mushrooms require natural light and airflow for proper cap formation and color creation.

Chapter 3

Growing on Straw

Straw is a standard substrate for many mushrooms. Some species, like oysters, grow well in straw, whereas others, like wine caps, will grow in straw but like some soil connection. Straw is readily available, is easily pasteurized and inoculated, and can be placed in any type of container, including regular gardening pots.

The Basics

Organic grain straw such as barley, oat, or wheat is available at most feed stores or garden centers and is an easy medium for mushroom mycelium to colonize. Be aware, though, that people with a hay, pollen, or wheat allergy may react to straw. Once colonized, getting mushrooms to grow and fruit well on straw can be a bit trickier. Pink and yellow oyster varieties and one strain of shiitake do quite well with straw. Wine caps, on the other hand, prefer straw to be combined with soil for indoor growing, or soil and leaves for outdoor growing.

Straw used for mushroom growing should be less than one year old and stored away from moisture. Avoid buying a straw bale that smells musty or has gray or black spots, an indication of mold and fungus spore contamination. Opt instead for a bale that is pale gold or pale gold with green tones and a slightly sweet hay or grain scent.

Straw works best if chopped before pasteurizing, cooling, and inoculating. For indoor growing quantities, a pair of scissors or shears can work. For larger growing operations, a weed whacker in a large barrel or within an enclosed space is a good option. That said, mushrooms can also be grown on a whole straw bale, if you prefer not to chop.

Pink Oyster Mushroom Cultivation

Pink oyster mushrooms, *Pleurotus djamor* or *Pleurotus flabellatus,* are among the most aggressive colonizing oyster mushrooms. They have a beautiful pink-to-red tone and fruit best in temperatures over 80°F. They will outcompete, and sometimes consume, molds and other fungi mycelium. In ideal growing conditions, pink oyster mushrooms can colonize and fruit in 14 days, sometimes less.

These mushrooms are so beautiful, they could almost be mistaken for flowers. Their seafood flavor is slightly stronger than that of some other oyster mushroom varieties and can be reminiscent of lobster, making them not only visually appealing but a great gourmet mushroom, too.

What You'll Need

Dust mask for handling non-wetted straw

Work or gardening gloves for handling the pre-pasteurized straw

Fresh organic barley, oat, or wheat straw (one bale weighs about 30 pounds and should fill 2 to 3 five-gallon buckets, or 20 to 30 one-gallon zip-top plastic bags). For those with a gluten or wheat allergy, I recommend oat straw to avoid reactions with the straw while working with it.

Shears, heavy-duty scissors, or a weed whacker

A large pot with a steam insert, or other vessel for pasteurizing the straw

Water

Heat source, like a stove or outdoor propane burner. Although you can pasteurize indoors, doing so outside may be the better option because of the steam.

Sponge

Surface disinfectant or cleaner

Heavy-duty, heat-resistant gloves (clean) for handling pasteurized straw

Tongs, for retrieving the straw out of the pot

Large wooden or metal spoon

A flat, water-safe work surface, like a large plastic table

Sawdust spawn or grain spawn for pink oyster mushrooms. If using an entire straw bale, you'll need approximately 5 pounds of spawn.

Tablespoon measure (clean)

Containers such as heavy-duty plastic bags, 1-gallon or 5-gallon buckets, or plant pots

Breathable tape (optional)

Plastic wrap, if using plant pots for growing

Greenhouse or mini-greenhouse if outdoors

Grow-tent if indoors. Use clear plastic bags or heavy-duty plastic and duct tape. Tape the plastic around a shelf, covering all interior surfaces except a loose flap at the front (for access to the grow-tent and added light, if desired).

A heavy-duty box cutter or multipurpose knife

Prepare the Medium

1. Wear a dust mask and work gloves when working with the straw and when chopping.

2. Evaluate your straw. Is it fresh, golden, and sweet-smelling? If you notice any hint of black powdery spots, dampness, or mustiness, choose a different bale. Make sure to check the underside, too.

3. Open the straw bale and take out a flake (a segment). The average straw bale has 10 to 12 flakes.

4. Using shears or heavy-duty scissors for smaller amounts or a weed whacker for larger quantities, cut, crush, or shred the straw into shorter pieces, 1 to 4 inches long.

continues

5. Fill a large pot halfway with water and bring to a boil over high heat. You could use a steamer in the pot.

6. Add the straw to the boiling water and simmer for at least 40 minutes for full pasteurization.

7. Wipe down your work surface with disinfectant.

8. Take off the gloves and set them aside in a separate location. Put on a new pair of clean, heavy-duty, heat-resistant gloves.

9. Using tongs, pull the straw out of the water and press the wet straw against a large wooden or metal spoon to squeeze some of the water back into the pot.

10. Place the pasteurized straw onto the work surface.

11. Spread out the straw and let it cool. If you need more straw, continue the pasteurization process until you have enough for your desired containers. For an average 5-gallon bucket, use at least 4 to 6 flakes of pasteurized straw. The average 1-gallon zip-top bag will hold about ⅓ flake (about 1 pound) of chopped, shredded, and pasteurized straw.

12. Let the straw cool to below body temperature. Straw that is too hot can kill the mushroom spawn.

Inoculate

1. Once the straw is cool to the touch, have your mushroom spawn ready.

2. Pack a 1-inch layer of straw in the bottom of your container.

3. Sprinkle about 1 tablespoon of spawn over the straw.

4. Repeat the layer of straw and spawn until the container is full. You should add about 10 percent spawn, by weight, to your desired container for the best colonizing results.

5. If using plastic bags, poke three to five small air holes at 2- to 3-inch intervals around the bag. If using buckets, cut or drill holes a handsbreadth apart around the container. Create at least one drain hole in the bottom of the container. Choose pots with at least one drain hole at the bottom.

6. Cover any holes in the containers except the bottom drain holes with breathable tape, if using.

7. Tie the plastic bags shut, secure the lids on the buckets, or cover the pots with plastic wrap. Do not block the bottom drain hole.

Colonize

1. Set aside your spawned substrate in a warm area between 64 and 86°F. Pink oyster mushrooms will colonize quickly, even compared to other oyster mushroom varieties.

2. Wait five days, then begin to check them daily for mycelium.

3. Once the substrate appears to be fully mycleated, remove the breathable tape if you used it, and place the container in a prepared area for fruiting (such as a greenhouse or mini-greenhouse for outdoor growing or a grow-tent for indoor growing).

Fruit and Harvest

1. Maintain a temperature for the mushrooms between 80 and 100°F.

2. Mist with water around the bags, buckets, or pots at least once per day. If your climate is dry and hot, however, mist two or three times per day to promote ideal humidity levels.

3. After a day or two, you should start to see pins forming by the ventilation holes. Keep misting, particularly in those areas.

4. After another two days, the mushrooms should be well formed and getting close to prime.

5. Harvest the mushrooms before their edges start turning upward and they begin releasing spores, or when the largest mushroom in the bunch is 2 to 3 inches across the cap.

6. Pink oyster mushrooms form in fairly large hands. Using a box cutter or multi-purpose knife, cut the mushrooms off close to where the mushrooms emerge from the growing medium.

7. Let the mushrooms dry and refrigerate them in a paper bag if you're not immediately using or preserving them.

8. After the first flush, soak or thoroughly mist your mushroom bags, buckets, or pots to encourage a second flush of mushrooms, which should appear within a week or two.

Shiitake "Straw" Strain Mushroom Cultivation

Although most shiitake mushrooms prefer to grow on hardwoods, one strain has been selectively cultivated and adapted to grow on straw. This strain will grow more slowly on straw than oyster mushrooms, but the straw substrate is easier than hardwood logs. Spawn for the straw strain shiitake should be available as grain spawn, which will transition well to continued straw growing.

Preparing shiitakes to grow on straw will require a little care that includes adding a bit of gypsum to ensure the mushrooms get the nutrients they need. Though other supplements are available, gypsum will give the best result for a home grower and has the lowest chance of cross contamination.

Shiitakes require more of a time commitment than oyster mushrooms because of their slower mycelium growth and fruiting time. From inoculation to harvest can take two to three months, and these mushrooms require daily checking at fruiting time.

What You'll Need

Dust mask for handling non-wetted straw

Work or gardening gloves for handling the pre-pasteurized straw

Fresh organic barley, oat, or wheat straw. Try to get the same straw type as your grain spawn for the easiest colonization. (One bale weighs about 30 pounds and should fill 2 to 3 five-gallon buckets, or 20 to 30 one-gallon zip-top plastic bags.)

Shears, heavy-duty scissors, or a weed whacker

A large pot with a steam insert, or other vessel for pasteurizing the straw

Water

Heat source, like a stove or outdoor propane burner. Although you can pasteurize indoors, doing so outside may be the better option because of the steam.

Sponge (clean)

A flat, water-safe work surface, like a large plastic table

Surface disinfectant or cleaner

Heavy-duty, heat-resistant kitchen gloves for handling pasteurized straw

Tongs

Long wooden or metal spoon

Grain spawn for the straw strain of shiitake. An entire straw bale will require about five pounds of spawn.

Gypsum. Use 2 to 10 percent by weight of dry substrate. An entire bale would require 0.6 to 3 pounds of gypsum. I recommend working with the smaller amount.

continues

Heavy-duty plastic bags (zip-top not necessary but must be able to tie shut)

Grow-light

Breathable tape (optional)

Greenhouse or mini-greenhouse, if outdoors

Grow-tent, if indoors. Use clear plastic bags or heavy-duty plastic and duct tape. Tape the plastic around a shelf, covering all interior surfaces except for a loose flap at the front (for access to the grow-tent and added light, if desired).

A heavy-duty box cutter or multipurpose knife

Prepare the Medium

1. Wear a dust mask and gloves when working with the straw and when chopping.

2. Evaluate your straw. Is it fresh, golden, and sweet-smelling? If you notice any hint of black powdery spots, dampness, or mustiness, choose a different bale. Make sure to check the underside, too.

3. Open the straw bale and take out a flake (a segment). The average straw bale has 10 to 12 flakes.

4. Using shears or heavy-duty scissors for smaller amounts or a weed whacker for larger quantities, cut, crush, or shred the straw into shorter pieces, 1 to 4 inches long.

5. Fill a large pot halfway with water and bring to a boil over high heat. You could use a steamer in the pot.

6. Add the straw to the boiling water and simmer for at least 40 minutes for full pasteurization.

7. Wipe down your work surface with disinfectant.

8. Take off your work gloves and put them aside in a separate location. Put on a new pair of clean, heavy-duty, heat-resistant gloves.

9. Using tongs, pull the straw out of the water and press a large wooden or metal spoon to squeeze excess water into the pot.

10. Place the pasteurized straw onto the work surface.

11. Spread out the straw and let it cool. For an average 5-gallon bucket, use at least 4 to 6 flakes of pasteurized straw. The average 1-gallon zip-top bag will hold about ⅓ flake (about 1 pound) of chopped, shredded, and pasteurized straw.

12. Let the straw cool to below body temperature. Straw that is too hot can kill the mushroom spawn.

Inoculate

1. Once the straw is cool to the touch, have ready your mushroom spawn and gypsum.

2. Mix the gypsum into the prepared straw.

3. Pack a 1-inch layer of the gypsum and straw mixture in the bottom of the plastic bags.

4. Sprinkle about 1 tablespoon of spawn over the straw.

5. Repeat the layers of straw and gypsum until your container is full. Add 10 to 15 percent spawn, by weight, to the plastic bags for the best colonizing results.

6. Poke three to five small air holes at 2- to 3-inch intervals around the bags, with one acting as a drain hole at the bottom.

7. Cover all the holes except the drain hole with breathable tape, if using.

8. Tie the plastic bags shut. Do not block the bottom drain hole.

Colonize

1. Set aside your spawned substrate. Straw shiitakes like colonizing in moderate temperatures, 70 to 80°F. Using a grow-light, make sure the mushrooms get 12 hours of light and 12 hours of darkness each day for best colonizing and fruiting.

2. Check every second or third day. Shiitakes will take one to two months to fully colonize.

3. Once the substrate appears to be fully mycelated—the normally white mycelium will turn light brown—remove the breathable tape, if you used it, or fully unwrap the growing blocks in the plastic bags, and place the mushrooms in a prepared area (such as a greenhouse or a grow-tent) for fruiting.

Harvest

1. For straw shiitakes, lower their ambient growing temperature to 60 to 66°F, and possibly add a humidifier to keep the humidity around 90 percent.

2. If you are not using a humidifier, mist the shiitakes with water, one to five times a day.

3. Fruiting should occur in three to seven days of changing the humidity and temperature.

4. Watch when the pins form. After another two days, the mushrooms should be well formed and getting close to prime.

5. Harvest shiitakes when they are 2 to 3 inches across the cap. Using a box cutter or multipurpose knife, cut or pull off the mushrooms close to where they emerge from the growing medium.

6. After the first flush, soak your mushroom substrate in cool water for 12 hours to encourage a second flush of mushrooms within a week or two.

❧ TROUBLESHOOTING ❧

There is no sign of mycelium growing after a week (oyster) to a month (shiitake); visible spawn has no mycelium growing into the substrate.

Warmer-than-body-temperature straw likely killed the spawn. Restart the process with fresh spawn and a new substrate.

Black or gray mold is forming on the straw around the edges of the container.

Your straw was either not fully pasteurized or was contaminated when you purchased it. Black mold is the most common fungi type if the straw was stored, harvested, or baled damp. Gray mold indicates contamination of the substrate after inoculation or pasteurization. Restart the process with fresh spawn and a new substrate.

The straw is fully colonized but after humidity and temperature changes, the pins don't form into full mushrooms.

The culprit in this situation may be too many fruiting holes or too much room to fruit. Soak the substrate in cool water, wrap in plastic wrap, and poke a limited number of holes (no more than five) where the youngest or newest pins have formed. Wait a few days and see if the mushroom will fruit properly.

Mycelium was colonizing nicely, but a thick yellow liquid is now in the bottom of the container; the mycelium is no longer thriving and seems resistant to fruiting.

The yellow liquid is part of the mushroom colonizing process. The issue is likely drainage. Make sure that the container is not sitting in standing water and that there is at least one drain hole at the bottom of the container. Once the excess liquid is drained off, the mycelium should recover its vigor.

continues

continued

The mushroom caps lack color, look misshapen, or are otherwise inconsistent with species norms.

Make sure the mushrooms, during colonization and fruiting, have 12 hours of light and 12 hours of darkness. You can have more hours of light than of darkness, but not more hours of darkness than of light. Light is necessary for color and cap formation.

Mycelium growth started vigorously but now has slowed or stopped, and the container is not fully colonized. There's no sign of fruiting.

Check the moisture content and humidity levels. Mushroom mycelium typically stops growing with a lack of water; less frequently, the problem is too much water or too many chemicals in the water. Use filtered water for misting your mushrooms if you are in a location where chloramine, chlorine, or fluoride is in the water.

The fruiting mushrooms are all stems, and the caps are small or misshapen.

Improve the ventilation and make sure the mushroom containers are not fully sealed. Mushrooms give off carbon dioxide and need fresh air for proper fruiting. With carbon dioxide levels too high, mushrooms will be all stem and no cap.

Chapter 4

Growing on Sawdust and Wood Chips

The majority of the cultivated gourmet mushrooms—including lion's mane, oyster, reishi, and shiitake—grow best when in contact with wood, especially hardwood sawdust, wood chips, or wood logs. Sawdust has the added benefit of allowing variation in the size of the fruiting block (inoculated substrate solid with mycelium where mushrooms will fruit). Most grow-kits use sawdust blocks.

The Basics

Because mushrooms prefer hardwoods—such as ash, beech, birch, or maple—be sure to avoid softwoods like pine and cedar. Wood chips are typically made from softwoods, so finding hardwoods may be your first challenge when working on the projects in this chapter.

Know any wood turners or woodworkers? Ask them to save hardwood shavings or sawdust for you. Just make sure what they give you stays dry until you can pasteurize it. Don't know anyone who works with wood? Purchase hardwood pellets for woodstoves (a 20-pound bag costs about $20). These pellets typically contain no added anti-fungals or chemicals that could negatively impact your mushroom growth.

In addition to the hardwood substrate, you'll need polypropylene (heat-resistant plastic) mushroom bags (for pasteurizing) and filters for this chapter's projects. Many of the wood-loving species grow slowly and need help avoiding bacteria, insect contamination, and molds.

Choose a protected shelf with some airflow for a growing area. You'll want to maintain the environmental humidity without causing water damage from condensation or standing water. A grow-light or modified grow-tent may also be useful for this purpose. A grow-tent can be created with open, clear plastic bags or heavy-duty plastic and duct tape. Simply tape the plastic around a shelf, making sure to cover all the interior surfaces, and close off all openings except the front. Leave the bottom of the front plastic flap loose to provide access to the grow-tent. If desired, add a grow-light.

Lion's Mane Mushroom Cultivation

Lion's mane mushrooms are a visually impressive mushroom with a unique seafood-like flavor. In the wild, lion's mane mushrooms fruit on hardwood trees, downed logs, and in damaged but living tree hollows. For a home-growing project, sawdust or hardwood chips is a good choice for this mushroom type. Lion's mane is a slower growing mushroom, so the added pasteurization and care for sawdust blocks also helps the mycelium flourish.

Expect four to six weeks from inoculation to the first flush. Lion's mane frequently produces only one large mushroom, although if you leave a bit of that mushroom attached to the substrate, it will grow a second fruiting body on top of the mushroom piece. The best results with lion's mane will be two to four medium-size mushrooms per block, per flush, though you can coax those mushrooms to double-grow before soaking the block to encourage a secondary flush.

This technique requires more focused hands-on start time than those in the previous chapter. Expect to dedicate at least two days to the setup and inoculation as well as several minutes a day to monitor the process before the first mushroom flush occurs.

What You'll Need

Hardwood sawdust, or hardwood chips or woodstove pellets. You'll use 5 cups for each 5-pound fruiting block.

A kitchen scale able to weigh up to 5 pounds

5-gallon plastic bucket (clean)

Water

Wheat bran from a health food store or baking supplier. You'll need 1¼ cups for each 5-pound fruiting block.

Polypropylene filter bags with built-in seal and filter for growing mushrooms

One-way filters for the polypropylene bags

Tyvek or other filter-type fabric

Large pressure canner with rack, able to maintain 15 pounds per square inch (psi) for 2½ hours. A 22-quart pressure canner should hold four fruiting blocks.

Ceramic plate that fits in the pressure canner without touching the sides

Still-air box. Make a still-air box with a 3-foot-by-2-foot cardboard box. Cut the top flaps off the box and tape clear plastic over these areas. Cut an opening on one side of the box, about 1 foot by 1 foot, and tape plastic over the top edge of that opening, so the plastic drapes like a curtain over the opening. Use this opening to place substrate bags, bring your spawn through, and add spawn to the substrate.

Kitchen gloves (clean)

Surface disinfectant or cleaner, at least 70 percent alcohol

Lion's mane grain or sawdust spawn; 12 ounces of spawn per 5-pound block of sawdust

Zip ties, one package

Grow-tent, if indoors. Use clear plastic bags or heavy-duty plastic and duct tape. Tape the plastic around a shelf, leaving a flap at the front for access.

Grow-light

Heavy-duty box cutter or multipurpose knife

Prepare the Medium

1. Decide how many 5-pound fruiting blocks you want to make.

2. Measure out the sawdust (or wood chips), using a ratio of 5 pounds of sawdust per 1 gallon of substrate, and place in the bucket. If using pellets, use a ratio of 5 cups of pellets per 1 gallon of substrate.

3. Add 6⅓ cups of cold, warm, or hot water per 5 pounds of sawdust to the bucket. I recommend using freshly boiled water to help mitigate cross contamination.

4. If using pellets, mix until they dissolve into sawdust, ensuring no solid pellets remain.

5. Add the wheat bran and mix until combined. Although bran helps increase the yield, adding too much also increases the chance of contamination, so stick with the recommended amount for your first growing experiment.

6. Using the kitchen scale, weigh out 4 pounds 4 ounces of substrate mixture and pack it into the polypropylene filter bag, making sure the sawdust doesn't cling to the sides. Repeat with additional mixture and polypropylene bags.

7. Pack the mixture down in each bag.

8. Fold over the top of the bag on its side gussets, so there is one fold between the mouth of the bag and the substrate. Put a piece of Tyvek in the mouth of the bag and smooth flat.

9. Fit the metal rack into the bottom of your pressure canner and place the bags on top. Depending on their size, four to six bags can be placed in the pressure canner, in two layers.

10. Fill the pressure canner with water to just barely reach the top of the lowest bag.

11. Place the ceramic plate on top to hold down the plastic bags and prevent the pressure release valve from becoming blocked.

12. Secure the pressure canner. Follow the canner's instructions to monitor steam, venting, and pressure.

13. Pressurize to 15 pounds per square inch for 2 to 2½ hours. Let the pressure release naturally before attempting to remove the top from the pressure canner.

14. Let the bags cool for at least 8 hours before proceeding with the inoculation.

Inoculate

1. Use a still-air box to facilitate inoculation and help reduce the chance of contamination. Alternatively, use clean kitchen gloves and thoroughly sanitize all surfaces before beginning. Make sure no pets are in the room and that air conditioners and fans are turned off.

2. Sterilize a kitchen scale with disinfectant spray. Weigh out 12 ounces of lion's mane grain or sawdust spawn and pour into the top of your first sterilized bag.

3. Close the bag with a zip tie.

4. Gently agitate the bag to encourage the spawn to drop down into your prepared substrate.

5. Make sure the filter is set in place, to allow the air exchange needed for the mushroom mycelium to grow.

6. Place the inoculated and prepared bag into your grow-tent or greenhouse.

7. Repeat the above steps for all sterilized bags.

8. Store any remaining spawn in the refrigerator for up to three months until you have time to create more sawdust bags.

Colonize

1. Lion's mane mushrooms prefer colonizing temperatures of 65 to 75°F and humidity of 80 percent or higher.

2. Monitor the blocks in your growing chamber and alternate cycles of 12 hours of light and 12 hours of darkness to encourage the mycelium to colonize.

3. The average sawdust block will be fully colonized in 10 to 21 days. Lion's mane mycelium is finer and thinner than other mushroom mycelium, so full colonization may not be as obvious.

4. When pins start forming, begin to prepare for fruiting and harvest.

Harvest

1. With the appearance of the first pins, lower the temperature by 5°F in your grow-tent.

2. Cut three to five small X's in the plastic over the pins to get medium-size mushrooms.

3. As the pins grow, make sure to mist them with water at least once per day.

4. Harvest when the mushroom has well developed "teeth" (the sort of furry appearance of these mushrooms) and is about the size of a clenched fist. It should take three to five days to reach that size.

5. If the mushrooms start turning yellow or pink, harvest them even if they haven't reached the expected size. They are supposed to remain white.

6. Cut off the mushrooms close to the growing medium with a box cutter or multi-purpose knife, making sure to leave some of the mushroom attached. It will grow a second fruit in the same place as the first.

7. Brush any visible dirt off the mushrooms and store them in a paper bag in the refrigerator for up to two weeks. Lion's mane mushrooms can be dried and reconstituted.

Reishi Mushroom Cultivation

Reishi mushrooms are a medicinal mushroom variety and can be grown on most hardwoods. One variety of reishi, the hemlock reishi, will grow on softwoods. Sawdust blocks permit the most control of the reishi substrate as well as a higher level of control and monitoring of the reishi fruiting bodies.

Reishi mushrooms are decent colonizers that take six to nine months to fully grow from antlers to full conks. They are a woody mushroom with very little flesh, so they are normally used in teas, tinctures, and broths, or as powders.

Some growers recommend burying fully colonized blocks of reishi spawn in soil in a small garden bed or a large planter pot to help the mycelium maintain their moisture. Others recommend simply harvesting the antlers as they get long enough without trying to grow full-size conks. Enjoy experimenting and finding out what works best for you.

What You'll Need

Hardwood sawdust, hardwood chips, or woodstove pellets. You'll use 5 cups for each 5-pound fruiting block.

A kitchen scale able to weigh up to 5 pounds

5-gallon plastic bucket (clean)

Water

Wheat bran from a health food store or baking supplier. You'll need 1¼ cups wheat bran for each 5-pound fruiting block.

Polypropylene filter bags with built-in seal and filter for growing mushrooms

One-way filters for the polypropylene bags

Tyvek or other filter-type fabric

Large pressure canner with rack, able to maintain 15 pounds per square inch (psi) for 2½ hours. A 22-quart pressure canner should hold four fruiting blocks.

Ceramic plate that fits in the pressure canner, but does not touch the sides

continues

Still-air box. Make a still-air box with a 3-foot-by-2-foot cardboard box. Cut the top flaps off the box and tape clear plastic over these areas. Cut an opening on one side of the box, about 1 foot by 1 foot, and tape plastic over the top edge of that opening, allowing the plastic to drape down like a curtain over the opening. Use this opening to place substrate bags, bring your spawn through, and add spawn to the substrate.

Kitchen gloves (clean)

Surface disinfectant or cleaner, at least 70 percent alcohol

Reishi mushrooms grain or sawdust or grain spawn 12 ounces of spawn per 5-pound block of sawdust

Zip ties, one package

Grow-tent, if indoors. Use clear plastic bags or heavy-duty plastic and duct tape. Tape the plastic around a shelf, covering all interior surfaces except for a loose flap at the front (for access to the grow-tent and added light, if desired).

Grow-light

Large plant pot (optional)

Potting soil (optional)

Mini-greenhouse (optional). Construct by covering the pot with plastic and taping shut.

Heavy-duty box cutter or multipurpose knife

Prepare the Medium

1. Decide how many 5-pound fruiting blocks you want to make.

2. Place 5 pounds of sawdust or wood chips or 5 cups of pellets into the bucket.

3. Add 6⅓ cups of cold, warm, or hot water per 5 pounds of sawdust. I recommend using just boiled water to help mitigate cross contamination.

4. If using pellets, mix until they dissolve into sawdust, ensuring no solid pellets remain.

5. Add the wheat bran and mix until combined. Although bran helps increase the yield, adding too much also increases the chance of contamination, so stick with the recommended amount for your first growing experiment.

6. Using the kitchen scale, weigh out 4 pounds 4 ounces of substrate mixture and pack it into the polypropylene filter bag, making sure the sawdust doesn't cling to the sides. Repeat with additional mixture and polypropylene bags.

7. Pack the mixture down in each bag.

8. Fold over the top of the bag on its side gussets, so there is one fold between the mouth of the bag and the substrate. Put a piece of Tyvek in the mouth of the bag and smooth flat.

9. Fit the metal rack into the bottom of your pressure canner and place the bags on top. Depending on their size, four to six bags can be placed in the pressure canner, in two layers.

10. Fill the pressure canner with water to just barely reach the top of the lowest bag.

11. Place the ceramic plate on top to hold down the plastic bags and prevent the pressure release valve from becoming blocked.

12. Secure the pressure canner. Follow the canner's instructions to monitor steam, venting, and pressure.

13. Pressurize to 15 pounds per square inch for 2 to 2½ hours. Let the pressure release naturally before attempting to remove the top from the pressure canner.

14. Let the bags cool for at least 8 hours before proceeding with the inoculation.

Inoculate

1. Use a still-air box to facilitate inoculation and help reduce the chance of contamination. Alternatively, use clean kitchen gloves and thoroughly sanitize all surfaces before beginning. Make sure no pets are in the room and that air conditioners and fans are turned off.

2. Sterilize a kitchen scale with disinfectant spray. Weigh out 12 ounces of reishi mushroom grain or sawdust spawn and pour into the top of your first sterilized bag.

3. Close the bag with a zip tie.

4. Gently agitate the bag to encourage the spawn to drop down into the prepared substrate.

5. Make sure the filter is set in place, to allow the air exchange needed for the mushroom mycelium to grow.

6. Place the inoculated and prepared bag into the grow-tent.

7. Repeat the above steps for all the sterilized bags.

8. Store any remaining spawn in the refrigerator for up to three months until you have time to create more sawdust bags.

❧ GROWING ON TOILET PAPER ❧

If you have a small quantity of spawn leftover from one of your projects, try growing it out on toilet paper! Oyster spawn is the best mushroom variety for this kid-friendly project because of its speedy colonization. You only need a roll of toilet paper, boiling water, and mushroom spawn. Pour boiling water over the toilet paper roll, until it's thoroughly soaked. Let the water drain and the paper cool. Place the roll in a clean plastic bag, pull out the center cardboard tube, and fill the center hole with spawn. Seal the bag, and let the spawn colonize. Open the bag to air once every three days to ensure even growth. Once mycelium is visible on all surfaces of the toilet paper roll, the colonization is complete. Remove the paper from the bag and mist two or three times a day in a lighted place until mushrooms form. Open the top of the bag to preserve humidity if your home is dry. Harvest the mushrooms when they reach full size.

Colonize

1. Reishi mushrooms prefer colonizing temperatures of 60 to 80°F.

2. Monitor the bags in your growing area and alternate cycles of 12 hours of light and 12 hours of darkness to encourage the mycelium to colonize.

3. Reishi mycelium will colonize rapidly over the course of one month. Once the fruiting blocks are fully covered in mycelium, watch for antlers to appear at the tops of the blocks.

Harvest

1. Once antlers appear you have two choices: Let the reishi mushrooms fruit from the block, or bury the fruiting blocks in a small amount of potting soil in a large gardening pot for a more traditional fruiting method.

2. For in-bag fruiting, cut off the top of the bag once the antlers reach 3 to 6 inches in length.

3. Mist the open top of the bag daily with water, or twice daily if the antlers are quite dry. The antlers should begin to open and form conks.

4. As the conks grow, watch for the formation of a dusty powder, or for the white edge of the conk to begin to shrink. Once these two indicators appear, harvest your conks by cutting them from the fruiting block with a box cutter or multipurpose knife.

5. For buried fruiting, remove the fruiting block from the plastic bag and place on some soil in a large gardening pot. Cover the sides and top lightly with soil, and water thoroughly.

6. Make a mini-greenhouse out of clear plastic over the top of the pot and keep the container shaded. The plastic will help maintain the proper humidity.

7. Mist daily with water. The first antlers will die back, but secondary antlers should begin to form conks within one week.

8. When the white edges of the conks begin to shrink and a fine dusting of spores appear, it's time to harvest.

9. Using the box cutter or multipurpose knife, cut off the mushrooms near where they emerge from the growing medium.

❧ TROUBLESHOOTING ❧

The reishi antlers are not widening into conks.

This problem is more likely to happen if you've left the substrate inside the plastic bag. The form of the bag may allow the antlers to grow very long but prevent them from spreading into the proper conk shape. If the antlers have exceeded 6 to 8 inches and have been growing for at least a month, harvest them. You can still cut them up and dry them; they will have the same medicinal properties as the fully grown conk-shaped reishi, although your harvest will be lighter.

Mold is forming near the top of my substrate, but everything else appears to be well colonized.

Contaminated air got in while the substrate was cooling from pasteurization. In a well-ventilated room that is not your growing room, open the bag and use a sterile knife to cut the mold from the block. Discard the mold, along with any mycelium close to it. Reseal the bag and make sure the filter is in place. Return the bag to the grow room. As long as mold does not appear again, the bag should fruit well.

Lion's mane has lots of small fruits that quickly discolor pink or yellow.

The number of fruits and discoloration indicate two issues. First, the fruiting block has too many fruiting points, with more—and smaller—mushrooms produced than the mycelium can support. Seal off some of the cuts in the plastic bag or re-cover the top of the bag, if open. Second, although discoloration can indicate maturity, the problem is more likely that the general humidity is too low. Soaking the fruiting block again, misting more frequently, not opening the growing area as frequently to check on the mushrooms, and reducing the dry heat sources in the vicinity can help improve the humidity levels. Discolored mushrooms can still be harvested and used for culinary purposes, but use them immediately rather than preserving them.

Chapter 5

Growing on Compost

The most widely familiar mushroom species, the white button or agaricus and the wine caps, are grown on compost or sterile manure. Although the compost-growing process can be a bit more involved than that on straw or wood chips, as this chapter shows, the principles and basic processes are similar. And don't panic! You won't have to make your own compost to grow mushrooms on this medium, although this chapter will show you how to do so, too.

The Basics

Both agaricus and wine cap mushrooms can grow on straw, but they need soil, compost, or manure to encourage fruiting and proper development. Although you can find pre-sterilized manure or compost for use as potting soil at some garden centers, you could also create and sterilize your own starter compost at home using jars, a pressure canner or cooker, or an oven-based pasteurization method.

Agaricus and wine cap mushrooms grown on compost produce a stronger odor than those grown on straw or sawdust. The projects in this chapter are best done on a balcony or in an area with plenty of air exchange.

If compost growing is not your preferred method, one alternative could be combining one part straw, one part clean and sterilized coffee grounds, and one-half-part sterilized soil. This mixture works best with a grain-based spawn or sawdust spawn. Another method, straw-bale gardening, involves cutting holes in straw bales and placing soil and a plant in the holes to grow as the bale decomposes. Chapter 6 also has information on growing mushrooms in mason jars using spore syringes for even another alternative (see pages 77 to 83).

Agaricus Mushroom Cultivation

Agaricus mushrooms are your standard grocery store variety, also known as white button and portabella. The difference between the two is that white buttons are often the first flush of the mushrooms and have a lighter cap color. The second flush often has a darker cap color and is sometimes permitted to grow larger, which is why you sometimes can find extra-large portabella mushrooms at the store for pizza and the like.

When you grow your own agaricus mushrooms, you can harvest them at your preferred size, eliminating the need to pay high prices for full-size portabella caps.

Traditionally, these mushrooms are grown in beds of pasteurized compost. For home growing, the easiest method is using an herb planter pot or a similar large container covered with plastic taped down to form a humidity tent.

These mushrooms will fruit out the top of a bucket as long as their substrate remains evenly damp. A light covering with clean straw can help when you want to encourage fruiting.

What You'll Need

Mushroom spawn for agaricus mushrooms, either a grain or sawdust spawn. Choose the spawn type labeled either white button or portabella.

Clean containers, such as ceramic herb growing pots. For this mushroom, pots are preferable to bags.

Plastic wrap

Compost or sterilized manure. Potting soil variations are usually pre-sterilized. Avoid "mushroom compost" potting soil, which has already been used for growing this species of mushroom and has nutrients that have broken down and been used up.

Well-ventilated area, preferably a balcony or garden space

Two old baking sheets for soil or compost pasteurization only

Disposable latex or neoprene gloves

Dust mask

Straw (optional); chopped and pasteurized

Coffee grounds (optional). If used within 24 hours of making coffee, grounds are usually sterile.

Pebbles for drainage at the bottom of the pot

Heavy-duty clear plastic bags to fit over your growing pots and act as mini-humidity tents

Prepare the Medium

1. Gather containers, spawn, and compost. This process is dusty, so work outdoors.

2. If working with already pasteurized or sterilized potting soil–type composts, check the bag for rips, tears, or other signs of cross contamination, and if needed, re-pasteurize the potting mix.

3. To pasteurize the potting mix, set your oven to 350°F. Spread 16 cups of potting compost onto a baking sheet and bake for 30 minutes. Remove from the oven and let the compost cool naturally.

4. Using filtered water or boiled and cooled water, dampen the pasteurized compost mix. The soil should be able to cling together when squeezed, but not be sopping wet or dripping.

5. Wear gloves to handle the pasteurized mixture.

6. Place a few pebbles or sterilized straw in the bottom of your herb pot to keep the mycelium away from any liquid that might pool there. Liquid is a natural by-product of mycelation, but you don't want to drown the mycelium.

7. Combine equal parts compost and pasteurized finely shredded straw to stretch the compost and to get a lighter, more easily colonized mushroom substrate.

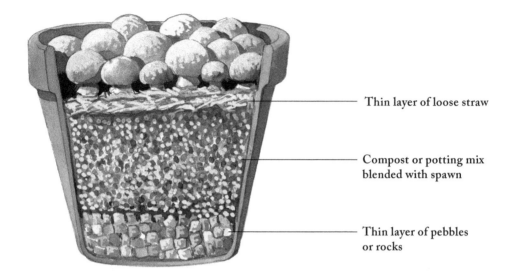

Thin layer of loose straw

Compost or potting mix blended with spawn

Thin layer of pebbles or rocks

Inoculate

1. When the dampened potting mixture is cool, combine 2 cups of sawdust or grain spawn with 16 to 20 cups of the potting mixture.

2. Wearing gloves and a dust mask, pack the mixture into a clean container.

3. Repeat these steps until all pots and spawn are used.

Colonize

1. Enclose each container in a heavy-duty clear plastic bag. Set aside in a lit area that does not receive direct sunlight.

2. In one to two weeks mycelium will appear on the insides of the pot and across the top.

3. Remove the plastic bag, and every day or every second day, mist the openings of the pot with water. Place a thin layer of loose straw across the top of the pot to help retain moisture.

4. When pins form, monitor the container closely for any sign of the caps beginning to open.

Harvest

1. White button mushrooms should be harvested when their caps are 1 to 2 inches across and the gills are still closed and covered. For portabella-style mushrooms, let the caps open about 50 percent before harvesting.

2. Many of these mushrooms will mature quickly, from pins to full spore-release, so once the pins form, monitor them and harvest before the caps open fully.

3. To harvest, simply grasp the base of the mushroom and pull; trim the end of the stem and set aside the mushroom to be washed before consuming.

4. Lightly rinse and dry the harvested mushrooms, then store in a brown paper bag in the refrigerator for up to one week.

5. Agaricus mushrooms are often consumed raw, although if you have any sensitivities to foods or the fiber in foods, you should cook all mushrooms, including agaricus species, before consumption. Most other mushroom varieties should be cooked before consumption regardless of any sensitivities.

Wine Cap Mushroom Cultivation

Wine caps are a favorite of many mushroom gardeners, partly because this species is one of the most aggressive and freely growing in an outdoor setting. For home cultivation, wine caps work well in smaller batches as long as they have some soil or compost contact. These mushrooms can be added to established outdoor gardens or even to small balcony garden beds. They will grow near other plants and will help increase the soil fertility. This mushroom's mycelium is unique in that it will consume soil nematodes, one of the more annoying microscopic garden pests that can destroy plant roots. Wine cap mycelium will also attract earthworms to outdoor gardens.

If you are growing on a balcony or in garden pots, use 5 to 10 percent spawn by weight per container to help ensure a thriving mushroom colony that is not cross contaminated by outdoor growing conditions.

What You'll Need

Clean containers, such as ceramic herb growing pots

Mushroom grain or sawdust wine cap spawn

Compost or sterilized manure. Potting soil variations are usually pre-sterilized. Avoid "mushroom compost" potting soil, which has already been used for growing mushrooms and could cross contaminate your substrate.

Disposable latex or neoprene gloves, 3 pair

Dust masks, one package

Baking sheet (if pasteurizing)

Well-ventilated outdoor area, preferably a balcony or garden space

Two old baking sheets for soil or compost pasteurization only

Water (if pasteurizing)

Pebbles or sterilized straw, for drainage at the bottom of the pot

Heavy-duty clear plastic bags to fit over your growing pots and act as mini-humidity tents

Plastic wrap

Straw (optional); chopped and pasteurized

Prepare the Medium

1. Gather your containers, spawn, and compost. This process is dusty, so work outdoors.

2. If using already pasteurized or sterilized potting soil–type composts, while wearing gloves and a dust mask, check the bag with the compost for rips, tears, or other signs of cross contamination, and if needed, re-pasteurize the potting mix.

3. To pasteurize the potting mix, set your oven to 350°F. Spread 16 cups of potting compost onto a baking sheet and bake for 30 minutes. Let the compost cool naturally. Remove the gloves you were wearing and set them aside. Put on new, clean gloves.

4. Using filtered water or boiled and cooled water, dampen the pasteurized compost mix. The soil should be able to cling together when squeezed, but not be sopping wet or dripping.

5. Place a few pebbles in the bottom of your container to keep the mycelium away from any liquid that might pool there. Liquid is a natural by-product of mycelation, but you don't want to drown the mycelium.

6. Combine equal parts compost and pasteurized finely shredded straw to stretch the compost and to get a lighter, more easily colonized mushroom substrate.

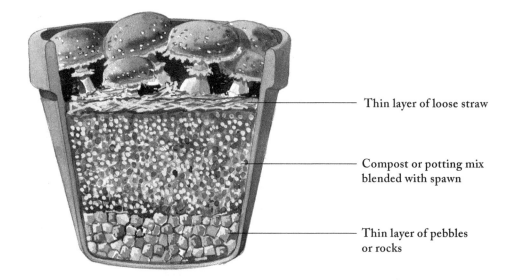

Thin layer of loose straw

Compost or potting mix
blended with spawn

Thin layer of pebbles
or rocks

Inoculate

1. When the dampened potting mixture is cool, combine 2 cups of the grain or saw-
    dust spawn with 16 to 20 cups of the potting mixture.

2. Wearing new, clean gloves and a dust mask, pack the mixture into a
    clean container.

3. Repeat these steps until all pots and spawn are used.

Colonize

1. Enclose each container in a heavy-duty clear plastic bag. Set aside in a lit area that does not receive direct sunlight.

2. In one to two weeks, mycelium will appear on the insides of the containers and across the tops.

3. Remove the plastic bags, and every day or every second day, mist the openings of the pot with water. Place a thin layer of loose straw across the top of the containers to help retain moisture.

4. When pins form, monitor the containers closely for any signs of the caps beginning to open.

Harvest

1. Wine cap mushrooms should be harvested before the caps are open fully and when they measure 2 to 3 inches across and still have a deep burgundy color.

2. To harvest, simply grasp the base of the mushroom and pull. The end of the stem can be trimmed and used to inoculate a new batch of compost or placed in a garden bed or by a wood-chip path to encourage mushrooms to naturalize in the area.

3. Lightly rinse off the harvested mushrooms and store them in a brown paper bag in the refrigerator for up to one week. Wine cap mushrooms can cause gastric upset, so only eat them cooked and do not consume them for more than three days in a row.

🌿 TROUBLESHOOTING 🌿

Mycelation is slow and no mycelium is visible on the sides or top of my container.

Make sure the growing medium is not too dry. Do a finger check at the top of the vessel and at any of the side holes. If the medium doesn't feel damp to a depth of at least one inch, water the pot from the top and from any side openings. If you are growing on a balcony, porch, or deck, the vessel may dry out faster than indoor grow bags.

There's a yellow liquid seeping from the bottom of my pot.

Yellow water-like liquid at the bottom of the pot or seeping from the bottom of a container may simply be the mycelium metabolizing and breaking down the substrate, a natural part of the process. Or, if you've had heavy rain and the vessel was not protected, the extra water may be seepage through the substrate. Some substrate combinations will naturally leach light-yellow- to dark-toned water when overwatered because of rain.

The mushrooms started to form, but blackened and fell off before growing to normal size.

Lack of moisture may be the culprit in this scenario. If the mushrooms lose humidity when pinning, the pins will not form into full mushrooms. Make sure the plastic over the container that's acting as a humidity tent remains closed and secured when you are not watering or checking the mushrooms. Another reason for blackened mushrooms forming and falling off could be exposure to direct sunlight, which could bake the mushroom pins. Be sure to keep your mushrooms away from direct sunlight. Still another possibility is there is too much space for and not enough strength in the mycelium, causing an overflush. Clear the dead pins from the surface of the pot, and close off 50 percent of the top or side openings. Water well and wait to see if a fresh flush begins.

The first flush went well, but a second flush is nowhere in sight even after several weeks.

The problem could be a temperature that is too hot outdoors for the mushrooms to flush, even if the humidity is right. Try bringing the vessel inside and out of the heat for a few days. You can also shock your mushrooms by watering with cool or cold water, letting the vessel drain in the sink, and placing it in a cool location with indirect lighting. This should be enough to start your flush.

Small flies are circling my mushrooms, and small larvae or grubs of some kind are in the gills.

Any mushroom growing outdoors will attract flies. To help prevent grubs, harvest the buttons as soon as the gill flaps start to separate from the stem and before the mushroom cap is fully open.

   If you missed a morning check and have fully open gilled mushrooms in the afternoon, you can still harvest and use them. Simply soak the mushrooms in lightly salted water for 20 minutes to drive out any larvae. Dry and store the mushrooms as normal.

A mushroom I didn't plant is growing out of my mushroom pot.

This likely means the substrate was not fully pasteurized. Do not eat a mushroom you don't recognize. However, try removing the mushroom and wait to see if your planted species ends up fruiting. If it does, you will still get a harvest. And for the future, remember to thoroughly pasteurize your substrate and let it cool before inoculation.

Chapter 6

Growing in Mason Jars

When growing mushrooms in jars, the goal is to make a solid mycelium brick and then fruit the brick outside the jar in a humidity-controlled fruiting tent. This method, which allows you to get started with spore syringes, is effective for nearly any mushroom species and is a great way to test new mushroom varieties without a lot of risk or material investment.

The Basics of Going Beyond the Basics

The traditional mason jar method, sometimes called the "PF Tek Method," is a quick low-tech technique that uses common tools for small-scale mushroom growing and can be adapted to any mushroom variety. However, this method is labor-intensive and is not known for high yields.

The PF Tek Method uses a grain-based substrate made from rye grain, brown rice flour, and gypsum sterilized in a pressure canner in mason jars. The jar lids are perforated and covered with aluminum foil for protection. Once the jars are cool from the sterilization process, a sterilized spore syringe is used to introduce three loads of suspended spores around the edge of the jar lid where it seeps into the prepared substrate. After a one- to two-week incubation period, a solid block of mycelium forms. The blocks are tapped out of the jars into a sterile growing area equipped with a humidity tent for fruiting. The blocks are then soaked to shock them into fruiting, and after each flush, they can be shocked again to encourage more mushrooms to grow. Each block should have two to five flushes of mushrooms, but the number of mushrooms per flush decreases with each subsequent flush.

Cordyceps Mushroom Cultivation

I prefer to use the mason jar method with one of our friendly medicinal mushrooms, the cordyceps species. Cordyceps is a slow-growing variety and can be challenging to grow. Because this method enables very small quantities of perfectly sterilized substrate to be inoculated using a spore syringe, it is ideal for this mushroom type.

Unlike with other mushroom species undergoing the PF Tek Method, the cordyceps are left in their jars throughout the whole growing process and the substrate fills only one-third to one-half of the jars. The extra space provides headroom for the antlers to grow.

What You'll Need

Straight-sided, wide-mouth mason jars with two-part metal lids and rings. Use the 1-pint size. Alternatively, use small straight-sided water glasses, but they require more care with the foil.

Hammer, for making air holes in the jar lids

Nail, for making air holes in the jar lids

Sandpaper, or a nail file (optional)

Rye grain; use 4 cups if using 12 (½ pint–size) jars

Brown rice flour; use 4 cups if using 12 (½ pint–size) jars

Vermiculite, which is a blend of mica and other minerals to help retain moisture in potting soils. Use 4 cups if using 12 (½ pint–size) jars, plus enough to add a ½-inch layer to each jar.

Water (preferably distilled)

A pressure canner or pressure cooker. Be sure to use a rack or jar rings to keep the jars from resting on the bottom.

Room with still air, a fume hood, or other clean and mostly sterile space. A bathroom could be a good choice.

Disposable latex or neoprene gloves

Dust mask

Surface disinfectant or cleaner

Sponge (clean)

Candle, for sterilizing using the flame

Matches or lighter

Spore syringe for cordyceps mushrooms

Box, grow-tent, or humidity tent, for fruiting blocks, or for monitoring the cordyceps environment

One-way filters, to place over jars

Multipurpose knife

Prepare the Medium

1. Sterilize the jars and lids by boiling them in water for five minutes.

2. Using the hammer and nail, punch three holes around the outer rim of the lids. Use sandpaper or a file to remove sharp metal edges from the punched holes, if desired.

3. Mix 1 part rye grain, 1 part brown rice flour, and 1 part vermiculite with enough water to dampen the mixture thoroughly; for a set of 12 (½ pint) jars, your mixture will be 4 cups each of rye grain, brown rice flour, and vermiculate, plus 3 to 4 cups of water.

4. Fill the jars half-full with the substrate mixture.

5. Add a ½-inch layer of non-dampened vermiculite to the top of the substrate mixture to act as a contamination barrier.

6. Screw the lids on the jars, secure with the rings, and cover with aluminum foil.

continues

7. Place the jars in the pressure canner (can be stacked) and fill the pot with enough water to come to the shoulders of the lowest jars.

8. Pressurize to approximately 15 pounds per square inch and leave in for 2 hours. Let the pressure release naturally and the canner cool naturally with the jars inside for at least 12 hours. Do not open the canner.

Inoculate

1. Wearing clean gloves and a dust mask, create a sterile space for inoculation. This can be a bathroom or other small room with no draft. Wipe down any surfaces with disinfectant and make sure pets stay out of the area.

2. Gather the candle, matches, spore syringe with needle, a box or grow-tent, and the still-closed pressure canner.

3. Light the candle. Take one jar out of the pressure canner. Heat the needle of the spore syringe to red hot over the candle.

4. Let the needle cool to visually neutral, take the lid off the jar, and inject 0.5 milliliter of spore in three spots for a total of 1.5 milliliters per jar.

5. Repeat with the remaining jars, sterilizing the needle in the flame before every third jar, or if it touches any non-sterile surfaces.

6. Place the inoculated jars in a humidity-controllable container that you can monitor, such as a box, grow-tent, or humidity tent (pot covered with plastic taped shut).

Colonize

1. Leave the jars in the container while colonization happens. Make sure there is some light and air exchange outside the jars to ensure the jars do not create too much carbon dioxide and slow the mycelium growth.

2. Monitor the jars on a daily or weekly basis to see if the mycelium is growing and to check for contamination. Any green, black, or pink coloration is an indicator of potential mold contamination. Contaminated jars should be removed and discarded. Be sure not to open potentially contaminated jars beside or inside your grow space.

3. Colonization is complete when the block of substrate appears to be solid, usually within one to three months.

Birth

1. Remove the lid, replace with a one-way filter, and screw on the ring.

2. Increase the humidity in the jar to turn it into a fruiting chamber. To do this, boil and cool water, then spray the area with this water and let it evaporate. Monitor the humidity and temperature while watching for pins to form. You may need to water the individual jars if they have dehydrated during colonization.

Fruit

1. Antlers should begin to form within one week of taking the lid off the jar but will take two weeks to one month to fully grow.

2. Monitor the moisture and air exchange throughout this time.

Harvest

1. Using a multipurpose knife, harvest the mushrooms when the antlers are about 2 inches long, or when they create an interesting shape that you like.

2. Slice and dry the mushrooms shortly after harvesting. Cordyceps are normally used in tea or broth, or they are ground to use for supplements.

❧ TROUBLESHOOTING ❧

There is black, green, or pink mold contamination in my jars.

The barrier layer of vermiculite was too damp or there was too much air exchange when adding the spores. Increase the vermiculite barrier layer and make sure you are poking the needle all the way through the barrier layer when inoculating. Add a protective layer of breathable tape over the inoculation holes as extra protection, if desired.

My jars cracked in the pressure canner.

Use a rack or barrier in the bottom of the canner to prevent spot heat transfer and ensure the jars won't damage while pasteurizing. Also, make sure the pressure has released naturally and completely before removing the pressure canner lid. Otherwise, you might end up with shattered jars.

My mushrooms are misshapen or the wrong color.

Air exchange is crucial for proper cap and stem formation as is diffuse natural light for proper cap formation. If the mycelium is grown without air exchange and in darkness, mushroom formation can be affected, though the mushrooms are still edible. For picture-perfect mushrooms, create a consistent air exchange in the fruiting chamber to remove carbon dioxide and bring in oxygen.

I got only one mushroom per flush.

It is very common to get only one to five mushrooms per block, per flush, and each subsequent flush will send up fewer mushrooms than the first. Cordyceps are likely to have three to five antlers per jar and may not give a second flush.

Colonization is slow or incomplete but pins are forming.

One reason for slow colonization is an overly damp substrate. Aim for one damp enough to hold together, but light enough to break apart if dropped. Use a medium grain vermiculite and a coarse-ground rice flour with the rye grains to help the substrate remain light enough for good colonization.

Another reason for slow colonization may be inadequate air exchange in the base of the jars, especially if you're using full-size pint jars, which prevent the mycelium from growing that deep. Use a smaller jar and ensure enough air exchange. Nail holes in the lid should provide enough gas exchange, unless the jar is too deep.

Delay using birthing jars, even if pins have formed, until substrates are fully colonized to avoid contamination or a false flush.

Part II

Fruits of Your Labor

Congratulations! Now that you have successfully culti-vated mushrooms, it is time to figure out how to prepare them for use. The following chapters present processing projects and techniques to help you store your mushrooms and recipes to help you enjoy your harvest to the fullest.

Chapter 7

Processing Projects

Your harvested mushrooms can be preserved in a number of ways, but I do not recommend canning. Although canned mushrooms are a grocery store staple, I find them to be rubbery. Choosing the method you will use depends on the variety of mushroom you're growing, the size of your mushroom flush, the number of substrates you're working with, and the amount of space and time available. The best part is you won't need specialized equipment.

How to Dehydrate

Dehydration, a mainstay of mushroom preservation, is most frequently used with cordyceps, lion's mane, reishi, and shiitake, as well as wild mushrooms like morels. Dehydration is also a pre-step for powdering mushrooms for use in broths, energy balls, medicines, and other applications.

To reconstitute dehydrated mushrooms, thoroughly rinse them to remove any lingering grit and soak them in a bowl filled with cool water for 12 to 24 hours. Drain, pat dry, and use them in your recipes as normal. Dense mushroom varieties—including lion's mane, reishi, and shiitake—dry and reconstitute best in comparison to other types. On the flip side, other varieties—including agaricus, oysters, and wine caps—don't reconstitute well from dried.

Some situations allow the mushrooms to reconstitute while cooking, such as when using a slow cooker. Still other mushrooms, cordyceps and reishi, don't need to be reconstituted, because they behave a lot like bay leaves—they give flavor to a dish but are not meant to be eaten.

Store dried mushrooms in glass jars with secure lids or in plastic zip-top bags and place them in a cool, dry place, out of direct sunlight. Dried mushrooms can keep up to two years with no loss of flavor.

Air Dry

Air and sun drying is a great method for increasing the vitamin D content of your mushrooms. Alternatively, rest them, gills up, in the sun for a few hours before using them in cooking or other preservation methods.

To air dry, set up a tray using a tea towel or piece of cheesecloth over a standard cooling rack that rests on a baking sheet to allow good airflow. Lay out the sliced mushrooms or small whole mushrooms onto the prepared tray. To sun dry, place the tray in the open, preferably direct, sunlight. If outdoors, put netting over the mushrooms to prevent bugs or birds from getting at them.

The air-and-sun-dry process will take two to four days. Bring outdoor trays inside at night to protect your mushrooms from dew and nighttime moisture.

Electric Dehydrator

A dehydrator is one of the easiest and most energy efficient ways to preserve your mushroom harvest. A standard dehydrator can hold several pounds of mushrooms and will dry them within 8 to 16 hours. To dry agaricus, oyster, or wine cap mushrooms, use a dehydrator.

To use the dehydrator, begin by making sure the trays are clean. Wash them if you notice visible dust or crumbs, or if you previously dried something flavorful like fruits or hot peppers. Rinse the mushrooms and cut them into ¼-inch slices. Small mushrooms and the thinner oyster mushrooms can often be dried whole. Place the mushrooms on the dehydrator trays, making sure they don't overlap.

Place the filled trays in the dehydrator and dehydrate at 150°F for two to three hours. Mushrooms should be crisply dried and you should be able to snap them cleanly with your fingers. If, when cooled, the mushrooms become leathery, they will need more drying time. Rotate the racks if you are using an older dehydrator with the fan in the back, and check that all mushrooms are completely dried when removing them from the dehydrator. Cool the mushrooms to room temperature before storing them in glass jars or zip-top plastic bags. Reconstitute or powder before using in cooking.

Oven Dry

Oven drying is one of the most accessible methods of dehydrating, although it is not as energy efficient as using a dehydrator or an air-and-sun-drying method. You'll need an oven that can be set to 200 to 250°F, and several parchment-lined baking sheets. Do a quick rinse of the mushrooms to remove grime and grit. Cut the mushrooms into thin slices, about ¼ inch thick, and lay them out in a single layer on the baking sheets. Place the baking sheets in the oven and bake for two to five hours or more, rotating every hour. Most ovens can dry two full baking sheets at once. Mushrooms are dry when they are crisp and you can snap them in half by hand.

Let the baking sheets cool in the oven. Store the mushrooms in glass jars or plastic zip-top bags. Add a sealed silica packet to the storage container to help prevent moisture buildup. Varieties with higher water content, like oyster mushrooms, will take longer to dry. Less watery mushrooms, like resihi or shiitake, will work best with this drying method.

🌿 MYSTERY MUSHROOMS 🌿

When growing mushrooms indoors in a controlled environment, you should have no worries or questions about the mushrooms you've grown. However, if you are growing in open ground or outdoors, you may get volunteer wild mushrooms or end up with mushrooms that look different from what you expect. Always double-check coloration, scent, shape, and spore print of your mushrooms when growing them in open ground. Many species will look different when they are new buttons compared to older caps. Research images or descriptions for all stages of the mushroom you've planted. Taking spore prints is a great way to identify mushroom varieties, is a fun way to simply learn more about your mushrooms, and can provide kids with a great introduction to mycology. Remember, if you have any doubts, don't consume the mushrooms or preserve them for later consumption. You don't want to have to call poison control or, worse, have to go to the emergency room.

How to Grind into Powder

Cordyceps and reishi mushrooms are often ground for medicinal purposes. Mushrooms that don't reconstitute well from dried are also ideal as a powdered additive for soups, stews, and mixing in as a ground meat extender. For powdering mushrooms, start with fully dried and crisp mushrooms.

For coarse grinding that retains some texture and body in the mushroom powder, use a standard blender or food processor. For medicinal powders to add to drinks, choose a fine grind by starting with a coarse grind from the blender, then finely powdering in a coffee grinder or spice grinder. Use a dedicated grinder for finely powdering mushrooms, if possible, to avoid melding spice or coffee flavors with them.

To grind the mushrooms, break them up with your fingers and place them in a food processor or blender. Pulse until the mushroom pieces resemble coarse bread crumbs. If you'd like fine powder, transfer the coarsely ground mushrooms to a coffee grinder or spice grinder and pulse in five-second bursts until the grind resembles flour. Transfer the powdered mushrooms to a glass jar with a lid and set aside for use in drinks, energy balls, and other applications. As long as the mushrooms are fully dry, overgrinding is not a concern, but be careful not to stress the grinder.

How to Freeze

If you don't have a dehydrator and want to avoid oven drying because of excess energy use, freezing mushrooms is a good preservation method. Frozen mushrooms only need to be thawed before use, and can be frozen ground, partially cooked, sliced, or whole. Freeze small mushrooms whole for use as garnishes in baked dishes.

Because of their high water content, most mushrooms will lose some body if frozen when raw. Denser mushrooms, like shiitake, tend to do better with freezing.

Always wash any grit from your mushrooms before processing for freezing. Then place whole or sliced mushrooms on a parchment-lined baking sheet and freeze solid. Remove the mushrooms from the baking sheet and place them in zip-top freezer bags or another freezer-safe container and return them to the freezer.

Most mushrooms—including agaricus, oyster, and wine caps—have a water content that is a bit too high to reconstitute well from frozen. A great option is to precook these mushrooms, such as by sautéing them in butter, before freezing.

A third freezer option is to first coarsely grind the mushrooms in your food processor. Portion out ½ to 1 cup of the ground mushrooms and freeze them in zip-top bags. These ground mushrooms can be used for meat extensions, adding to chili and thick soups, or using in dishes such as beef Wellington.

Label and date your frozen mushrooms and use them within six months.

How to Prep for Cooking

If you are growing your mushrooms completely indoors, cleaning them before cooking will be minimal. Simply brush off any visible dirt, trim the stem end, and, if needed, give them a light rinse in water just before cooking. Indoor grown mushrooms won't have issues with flies, so there is no need to soak them, which can damage some mushrooms, making them soggy and less suitable for cooking.

After brushing off any visible dirt, you can store most mushrooms in a paper bag in the crisper drawer of your refrigerator, where they will keep up to one week.

Mushrooms grown outdoors, such as mature agaricus or wine cap mushrooms, might attract flies. In this case, soak the mushrooms briefly in a saltwater solution and let them dry for an hour on a dish towel or paper towel to prevent sogginess before storing in the refrigerator. You can avoid the worry about outdoor flies by harvesting agaricus and wine cap mushrooms close to the button stage, before the gills fully open and the spore matures. If you have harvested young buttons, simply rinse them off under running water right before cooking, as you would with indoor grown mushrooms.

Chapter 8

Culinary and Medicinal Recipes

continues

Culinary and Medicinal Recipes

continued

Reishi Tea

Makes 2 cups ☙ Prep time: 5 minutes ☙ Cook time: 1 hour

GLUTEN-FREE / VEGETARIAN

This tea features the earthy tone of reishi mushrooms blended with the sweeter flavors of holy basil, orange peel, and peppermint. Prepare your tea with fresh or dried reishi pieces for the best results. Experiment with adding your favorite herbs—try chamomile, rooibos tea leaves, green tea, or rose petals—to soften the bitter notes of the reishi mushrooms.

1 teaspoon reishi pieces

½ teaspoon dried orange peel

1 teaspoon dried peppermint leaves

1 teaspoon dried holy basil

3 cups water

Honey or maple syrup, to sweeten

Cinnamon stick, for garnish (optional)

1. In a stainless steel or ceramic pan (no aluminum), place the reishi, orange peel, peppermint, and holy basil.

2. Add the water and bring to a boil over high heat.

3. Lower the heat to medium and cook at a slow simmer for 1 hour.

4. Strain the herbs and discard.

5. Pour the tea into mugs and sweeten to taste with honey. Garnish each serving with a cinnamon stick (if using).

6. Store any leftover tea in an airtight container in the refrigerator for up to 4 days.

Tip: To avoid honey or maple syrup, add ⅟₁₆ to ⅛ teaspoon dried stevia leaves for sweetness.

Cordyceps Tea

Makes 2 cups ✍ Prep time: 5 minutes ✍ Cook time: 1 hour

GLUTEN-FREE / VEGETARIAN

The sweet and lightly floral flavors of chamomile, cinnamon, and rose hips join nicely with the hearty notes from cordyceps mushrooms in this medicinal tea. Use fresh or dried cordyceps pieces for the best results.

1 teaspoon cordyceps pieces

1 teaspoon dried whole rose hips

1 teaspoon dried chamomile blossoms

3 cups water

Honey or maple syrup, to sweeten

Cinnamon sticks, for garnish (optional)

1. In a stainless steel or ceramic pan (no aluminum), place the cordyceps, rose hips, and chamomile blossoms.

2. Add the water and bring to a boil over high heat.

3. Lower the heat to medium-low and cook at a slow simmer for 1 hour.

4. Strain the herbs and discard.

5. Pour the tea into mugs and sweeten to taste with honey. Garnish each serving with a cinnamon stick (if using).

6. Extra tea can be refrigerated.

Tips: Holy basil, mint, peppermint, rooibos tea leaves, green tea, and other herbs are also great in this tea. Like with the Reishi Tea (page 97), substitute the honey or syrup with ¹⁄₁₆ to ⅛ teaspoon dried stevia leaves, if you prefer.

Adaptogenic Hot Chocolate with Cordyceps Mushrooms

Makes 16 cups ✦ Prep time: 10 minutes ✦ Cook time: 10 minutes

GLUTEN-FREE / NUT-FREE / VEGAN / VEGETARIAN

Enjoy the health benefits of cordyceps mushrooms blended with raw cacao and two adaptogenic herbs: ashwaganda and maca. You'll find that the heartiness of the mushrooms and herbs complements the bitterness of the cocoa. Use your choice of milk—including dairy-free varieties—to make this rich hot chocolate truly your own.

½ cup raw cocoa powder

¼ cup dried ground cordyceps mushrooms

¼ cup ashwaganda powder

¼ cup maca powder

½ cup coconut sugar

2 tablespoons ground cinnamon

1 teaspoon cayenne pepper (optional)

1½ cups milk, any fat, or dairy-free milk

1. In a clean, dry bowl, blend together the cocoa powder, dried cordyceps mushrooms, ashwaganda, maca, coconut sugar, cinnamon, and cayenne pepper (if using).

2. Pour the mixture into a wide-mouth 1-pint jar with a securely fitting lid. Affix a label with the date on the jar. Store at room temperature for up to one year.

3. To make one serving of the hot chocolate, warm up the milk of your choice in a saucepan set over low heat.

4. Add 2 tablespoons of the chocolate mixture and whisk until the milk begins to steam or slightly bubble, 5 to 8 minutes.

5. Pour into a large mug and serve hot.

Medicinal Reishi and Cordyceps Elixir

Makes 3 cups ✎ Prep time: 30 minutes, plus 1 month steeping ✎ Cook time: 30 minutes

GLUTEN-FREE / NUT-FREE / VEGAN

This mushroom elixir is well worth the effort and monthlong waiting period. Because mushrooms have compounds best extracted by alcohol or water, elixirs like this one are excellent ways to get the most flavor, health benefits, and immune support out of your homegrown mushrooms. Here, I use a two-level extraction and then blend the extracts to make a whole-mushroom medicine.

1½ cups dried reishi mushrooms, divided

1½ cups dried cordyceps mushrooms, divided

2 cups 190 proof or 95 percent alcohol, such as Everclear

3 cups boiled water plus ¼ cup room temperature water, divided

1. In a wide-mouth quart jar, place 1 cup of reishi mushrooms and 1 cup of cordyceps mushrooms.

2. Pour in the alcohol and cover the mushrooms.

3. Cover the jar and place in a cool, dark place for one month.

4. Shake daily for the month.

5. Strain the mushroom pieces out of the alcohol and reserve the liquid. This is a mushroom tincture.

6. In a large saucepan, place the remaining ½ cup of reishi mushrooms and remaining ½ cup of cordyceps mushrooms. Add the boiled water and bring the mixture to a boil over high heat.

7. Lower the heat to medium-low and simmer until the liquid is reduced by at least half, 10 to 20 minutes.

8. Strain out the mushrooms and retain the liquid. You should have no more than 1 cup.

9. Combine the liquid with the mushroom-infused alcohol. This will bring down the alcohol percentage, but it will still be shelf stable. Discard the mushrooms.

10. To serve, mix 1 teaspoon of the elixir with ¼ cup of room temperature water and drink.

11. The elixir can be stored in an airtight container at room temperature for at least two years.

Tips: Take with an earthy-flavored tea for the most enjoyment. The tincture itself can be taken straight, or blended with water, tea, or juice, if desired.

Pumpkin and Reishi Energy Balls

Makes 12 (2 balls per serving) ✄ Prep time: 30 minutes, plus 1 hour to chill

GLUTEN-FREE / VEGAN

These fun and tasty energy balls are great for quick breakfasts or snacking and offer a nutritional boost with an adaptogenic twist. Here, the earthy flavor of mushroom is balanced by the richness of chocolate, coconut, nuts, and spices.

1 cup chopped walnuts

2 tablespoons coconut oil

1 cup chopped dates

1 cup pumpkin or squash puree

¼ cup maca powder, gelatinized

¼ cup reishi mushroom powder

2 tablespoons chia seeds

1 tablespoon ground Saigon cinnamon

1 teaspoon ground ginger

½ teaspoon ground cardamom

½ cup dark chocolate chips

½ cup shelled pumpkin seeds

½ cup shredded unsweetened coconut, divided

1. In a heavy skillet, toast the walnuts over medium heat until they are fragrant, 3 to 5 minutes. Set aside to cool.

2. In a food processor, process the cooled walnuts on low until they turn into nut butter.

3. Add the coconut oil and continue processing on low until smooth.

4. Add the dates and pumpkin puree and process on low until smooth. The dough will be stiff.

5. Add the maca powder, reishi mushroom powder, chia seeds, cinnamon, ginger, and cardamom, and pulse until just blended.

6. Transfer the mixture to a bowl and fold in the chocolate chips and pumpkin seeds. The dough will be moist but not sticky.

7. In a 7-by-9-inch baking pan, spread half the coconut across the bottom of the pan and put the remaining half into a shallow bowl.

8. Roll 1 tablespoon of the mixture in your palms to form a 1-inch ball.

9. Roll the ball in the coconut in the shallow bowl until it is fully covered.

10. Place the finished ball in the baking pan on top of the loose coconut. Repeat with the remaining mixture, placing each finished ball into the pan. You should have 12 balls.

11. Cover the pan with plastic wrap and refrigerate for at least 1 hour before serving.

Tip: The energy balls can be stored in an airtight container in the freezer for up to four months.

Reishi Mushroom Broth

Makes 8 cups ✍ Prep time: 15 minutes ✍ Cook time: 8 hours

GLUTEN-FREE / NUT-FREE / VEGAN / VEGETARIAN

This simple broth has a rich flavor that is great on its own or can be used as a base for soups or ramen. Better yet, this recipe calls for vegetable scraps, which provide mineral benefits and reduce waste from vegetable skins and leaves that are normally discarded.

1 yellow onion, diced, or 1 cup onion trimmings and peels

1 tablespoon coconut oil (if using diced onion)

½ cup dried reishi pieces

1 cup chopped celery leaves

1 cup carrot trimmings

4 garlic cloves, chopped

3 sprigs fresh thyme or 2 teaspoons dried thyme

4 sprigs fresh parsley

1 teaspoon cracked black peppercorns

1 tablespoon tamari, low-sodium, or gluten-free soy sauce

8 cups water

1. In a skillet over medium-high heat, lightly sauté the diced onion in the coconut oil until just softened.

2. In a slow cooker, combine the reishi, celery leaves, carrot trimmings, garlic, thyme, parsley, peppercorns, and tamari.

3. Add the water, ensuring that it covers the mixture, and stir to combine.

4. Set the slow cooker on low and cook for 8 hours.

5. Pour the broth into a large bowl through a sieve and press the liquid out of the solids, especially the mushrooms, which may absorb a decent amount of liquid. Compost or discard the solids.

6. Serve the broth hot, or let it cool to room temperature and store it in tightly sealed jars in the refrigerator for up to one week or frozen for up to six months. Use the broth anytime for stock or broth in recipes.

Shiitake Mushroom Gravy

Makes 4 cups *&* Prep time: 10 minutes *&* Cook time: 20 minutes

NUT-FREE / VEGETARIAN

This full-bodied gravy is a delightful companion for turkey or pot roast. Shiitake mushroom gravy, which is vegetarian friendly, also pairs well with pasta, quinoa, or rice.

4 tablespoons (½ stick) butter, salted

2 cups coarsely ground shiitake mushrooms, fresh or frozen

¼ cup all-purpose flour or gluten-free flour

4 cups Reishi Mushroom Broth (page 104)

1 teaspoon fresh thyme, minced

Salt

Freshly ground black pepper

1. In a stainless-steel saucepan, melt the butter over medium-high heat. Add the mushrooms and sauté until they start to brown, about 5 minutes.

2. Add the flour and stir to combine. Cook for a few minutes, until the mixture just starts to brown. Slowly add 1 cup of broth, whisking continuously. Gradually add the remaining 3 cups of broth, whisking after each cup. Add the thyme and the salt and pepper, to taste.

3. Simmer for 5 minutes, stirring occasionally to meld the flavors, until the gravy is thickened and heated through.

4. Pour into a gravy boat and serve.

Tips: Use sliced shiitakes for a heartier gravy that can act as a main dish when served over rice or pasta. Use gluten-free flour in place of all-purpose flour to make this gravy completely gluten-free.

Lion's Mane Cream of Mushroom Soup

Servings 4 ✿ Prep time: 30 minutes ✿ Cook time: 30 minutes

GLUTEN-FREE / NUT-FREE / VEGETARIAN

This recipe is super flexible and can be used as a substitute in recipes for canned mushroom soup. Try changing out the type of mushroom according to what you have on hand. Here, lion's mane mushrooms add a unique sea flavor, faintly reminiscent of clam chowder.

¼ cup oil of choice or 4 tablespoons (½ stick) butter, salted
2 cups shredded fresh lion's mane mushrooms

¼ cup tapioca starch or flour
1 cup cold water
1 cup cold milk or cream
½ teaspoon dried onion
¼ teaspoon dried thyme

Salt
Freshly ground black pepper
Slices of crusty artisan bread (optional)

1. In a large skillet, heat the oil over medium-high heat.

2. Add the mushrooms and sauté until they are lightly browned and soft, about 5 minutes.

3. Whisk in the tapioca starch and cook, stirring frequently, until the mixture just starts to brown.

4. Slowly add the water, whisking constantly. Slowly add the milk, whisking constantly. Add the dried onion and thyme and cook, stirring occasionally, until the mixture thickens, 10 to 15 minutes. Add salt and pepper to taste.

5. Serve hot with bread (if using).

Tip: The soup can be stored in an airtight container and refrigerated for up to five days or frozen for up to two weeks without the cream separating.

Fried Oyster Mushrooms in Butter

Serves 2 to 4 ✑ Prep time: 15 minutes ✑ Cook time: 5 minutes

GLUTEN-FREE / NUT-FREE / VEGETARIAN

There's nothing better than a mushroom fried in butter. The sponginess of mushrooms makes them great at soaking up all that richness, and the butter itself is a great complement to the mushroom's hearty, almost meaty, flavor. This technique works well with nearly any soft mushroom, including button, lion's mane, oyster, portabella, and wine caps.

**2 tablespoons butter,
 salted**

**3 cups chopped
 oyster mushrooms**

1. In a skillet, heat the butter over medium-high heat until it begins to bubble. Add the mushrooms and sauté until browned and most of the liquid has evaporated, 5 to 7 minutes.

2. Serve as a side dish, over meat, or with eggs.

Tips: Cooking mushrooms this way helps evaporate some of their water content, which also is good preparation for freezing the mushrooms (lasting up to six months in the freezer). Fried mushrooms are also the first step to making several mushroom preparation recipes, like Lion's Mane Cream of Mushroom Soup (page 106).

Wine Cap Mushrooms in Wine Sauce

Serves 4 ✄ Prep time: 15 minutes ✄ Cook time: 15 minutes

GLUTEN-FREE / NUT-FREE / VEGAN / VEGETARIAN

Mushrooms in wine sauce are often served with red meat. These mushrooms have a gentler flavor than the standard button or portabella varieties, and they stand up well with such meats as lamb or goat. In this side dish, gentle spices like oregano and parsley help bring out the umami flavor of the wine cap mushrooms, which is also complemented by an extra splash of red wine.

2 teaspoons olive oil

4 cups sliced wine cap mushrooms

1 tablespoon chopped fresh basil leaves

1 tablespoon fresh oregano

2 tablespoons chopped fresh parsley

½ teaspoon coarse salt

¼ teaspoon freshly ground black pepper

1 tablespoon red wine, plus more if desired

1. In a skillet, heat the olive oil over medium-high heat. Add the mushrooms and sauté until tender, about 7 minutes.

2. Add the basil, oregano, parsley, salt, and pepper, and sauté for 2 or 3 minutes more to bring out the flavors.

3. Add the wine and cook until the liquid reduces, about 3 minutes. If the liquid cooks down too much, add another splash of wine.

4. Serve with a meat or bean dish.

Tip: Wine caps are a mild-flavored mushroom, so avoid cooking them with garlic, which will overwhelm their delicate flavor.

Quinoa Salad with Button Mushrooms and Reishi Broth

Serves 4 ✒ Prep time: 20 minutes ✒ Cook time: 30 minutes

GLUTEN-FREE / VEGAN / VEGETARIAN

This salad is a perfect side dish, though it stands on its own as a light main course. Quinoa has a higher protein content than many grains and the mild flavor serves to highlight the reishi broth and fresh mushrooms. Enjoy this dish warm or cold.

1 cup quinoa, rinsed

2 cups Reishi Mushroom Broth (page 104)

1 pound button mushrooms, chopped

2 celery stalks, chopped

2 carrots, grated

½ cup chopped macadamia nuts or sunflower seeds

¼ cup crumbled feta cheese (optional)

2 tablespoons olive oil

2 tablespoons balsamic vinegar

1. In a saucepan, mix the quinoa and mushroom broth together and bring to a boil over high heat.

2. Lower the heat to medium-low and simmer until the quinoa is tender, 15 to 20 minutes.

3. Add the mushrooms, celery, carrots, nuts, and feta (if using) and stir until combined.

4. Add the olive oil and balsamic vinegar and stir until well coated.

5. Serve cold or warm.

Tips: For a sweeter salad, add chopped fresh fruit instead of the celery and some dried cranberries or raisins. Omit the vinegar and use only olive oil or sesame oil, if you prefer.

Pesto-Stuffed Button Mushrooms

Serves 4 ✐ Prep time: 45 minutes ✐ Cook time: 30 minutes

GLUTEN-FREE / VEGAN

If you love the flavor of pesto, these stuffed mushrooms are well worth making. Serve them as a side dish, an appetizer, or even a meal on their own. The pesto is full of deliciousness and the mushrooms easily complement the aromatic basil, garlic, and hazelnuts.

½ cup hazelnuts
5 garlic cloves, peeled
1 bunch fresh parsley
14 ounces fresh spinach

½ cup hazelnut oil, plus more if needed
2 cups fresh basil

½ teaspoon salt
16 button mushrooms, stems removed

1. In a skillet over medium heat, lightly toast the hazelnuts. Set aside and let cool.

2. Place the cooled hazelnuts in a food processor and pulse until finely chopped. Transfer the nuts to a bowl and set aside.

3. Combine the garlic, parsley, spinach, and hazelnut oil in the food processor and pulse until the mixture is smooth.

4. Add 1 cup of the basil leaves and continue pulsing until well blended. Add the remaining basil leaves and pulse until well blended.

5. Add ¼ cup of the chopped hazelnuts and continue pulsing until well blended. The mixture should have a fine paste-like texture.

6. Add the remaining ¼ cup of the hazelnuts and the salt, and pulse until the mixture has a uniform, fine texture.

7. If the pesto is too thick to blend freely, add more hazelnut oil, 1 teaspoon at a time, until it blends smoothly.

8. Place the mushroom caps on a large serving tray with the cavities facing up. Spoon the mixture into the mushroom caps. Any leftover pesto can be stored in a tightly sealed jar in the refrigerator for up to one week.

9. Serve chilled.

Tips: If you are allergic to hazelnuts, replace the nuts with pumpkin seeds and use sesame oil instead of hazelnut oil. If you'd like a more traditional pesto, add ½ cup finely grated Parmesan cheese or other cheese of choice when blending the pesto in the food processor.

Hummus-Stuffed Portabella Mushroom Caps

Serves 4 ✧ Prep time: 30 minutes

GLUTEN-FREE / NUT-FREE / VEGAN

Hummus is a versatile dish and the addition of mushrooms makes it even better. Serve any leftover hummus with extra veggies for a light meal that will be ready in less than an hour.

1 (15.5-ounce) can (about 2 cups) chickpeas, drained and rinsed

3 garlic cloves, minced

2 tablespoons olive oil, plus more if needed

1 tablespoon freshly squeezed lemon juice, plus more if desired

2 tablespoons tahini

Salt

Freshly ground black pepper

16 portabella mushrooms, stems and gills removed

Cayenne pepper, for dusting

Chopped fresh parsley (optional)

1. In a blender, place the chickpeas, garlic, olive oil, lemon juice, and tahini and pulse in the blender or mash by hand, until smooth. Add more olive oil if the mixture is too thick.

2. Add salt and pepper to taste. Adjust the lemon juice, tahini, or garlic to taste, adding more if desired.

3. Place the mushroom caps with the cavities facing up on a large serving tray.

4. Fill each mushroom cap with about 2 tablespoons of the hummus.

5. Dust the tops with cayenne pepper and garnish with parsley (if using).

6. Serve at room temperature or chilled.

Tips: Try altering the flavors of the hummus by adding other Mediterranean spices such as basil, oregano, or za'atar. For a spicy hummus, mix in cayenne pepper, red pepper flakes, or ½ teaspoon finely chopped jalapeño peppers.

Stuffed Wine Caps

Serves 2 to 4 ✍ Prep time: 40 minutes ✍ Cook time: 20 minutes

GLUTEN-FREE / NUT-FREE / VEGETARIAN

The light flavors of the cheese and spices blend well with the flavor of the mushrooms. The sturdiness of the wine cap also lends itself to being stuffed. This dish is great as finger food, a light lunch, or an appetizer before a nice salmon dinner.

12 fresh wine cap mushrooms, just barely past button stage

1 tablespoon olive oil

1 large garlic clove, minced

1 (8-ounce) package cream cheese, softened

¼ cup grated Parmesan cheese

¼ teaspoon freshly ground black pepper

¼ teaspoon onion powder

¼ teaspoon cayenne pepper

Fresh parsley sprigs, for garnish

1. Preheat the oven to 350°F. Line a baking sheet with parchment paper or spray with cooking spray.

2. Clean and stem the mushrooms. Chop the stems finely.

3. In a large skillet, heat the oil over medium heat. Add the garlic and mushroom stems and cook until any moisture has disappeared, taking care not to burn the garlic. Set aside to cool for 5 minutes.

4. Add the cream cheese, Parmesan cheese, pepper, onion powder, and cayenne pepper and stir until combined. The mixture will be thick.

5. Using a spoon, fill each mushroom cap with the stuffing, mounding it over the top of each one. Arrange the mushrooms on the prepared baking sheet.

6. Bake for 20 minutes, or until the liquid is just starting to pool under the mushroom caps. (Wine cap mushrooms won't have quite as much liquid as button mushrooms.)

7. Garnish with parsley (if using) and serve.

Rice with Lion's Mane Mushroom Gravy

Serves 4 ✒ Prep time: 30 minutes ✒ Cook time: 45 minutes

NUT-FREE

This simple dish highlights the unique flavor of lion's mane mushrooms. Serve hot, or alternatively, toss the rice in the gravy and serve it cold, as a rice salad.

1 tablespoon olive oil

1 cup long grain wild rice

3 cups water

4 tablespoons (½ stick) butter, salted

2 cups shredded lion's mane mushrooms, fresh or frozen

¼ cup all-purpose flour

4 cups beef broth or mushroom broth

1 teaspoon fresh thyme, minced

Pinch freshly ground black pepper

Pinch salt

1. In a medium saucepan, heat the olive oil over medium-high heat. Add the wild rice and sauté until the rice starts to smell nutty, 2 to 5 minutes. Add the water and bring to a boil.

2. Lower the heat to medium-low and simmer until the rice splits and becomes fluffy, 30 to 45 minutes.

3. In a stainless-steel medium saucepan, melt the butter over medium-high heat. Add the mushrooms and sauté until they start to look wilted, about 5 minutes.

4. Add the flour and cook, stirring frequently, until the mixture just starts to brown. Slowly add 1 cup of broth, whisking continuously. Gradually add the remaining 3 cups of broth, whisking after each 1 cup addition. Add the thyme, pepper, and salt.

5. Simmer, stirring occasionally, until the sauce thickens, about 5 minutes.

6. Spoon the rice onto individual plates and top with the gravy. Serve hot.

Wine Cap Mushroom and Beef Stir-fry

Serves 4 ✐ Prep time: 45 minutes ✐ Cook time: 30 minutes

GLUTEN-FREE

This quick stir-fry is customizable and is an easy main dish that includes loads of healthy vegetables. I prefer to make this recipe with meat leftovers, though fresh meat, chicken, or tofu make great accompaniments as well.

1 tablespoon coconut oil or sesame oil

1 medium yellow onion, chopped

1 (½-inch) piece ginger, minced

3 garlic cloves, minced

1 pound thinly sliced beef

1 cup chopped broccoli

1 tablespoon soy sauce

2 celery stalks, chopped

2 bunches bok choy, chopped

1 cup chopped wine cap mushrooms

¼ cup whole almonds

3 tablespoons red wine

Hot cooked rice

1. In a large skillet or wok, heat the oil over medium-high heat. Add the onions, ginger, garlic, and beef and cook until the beef is browned and the onions are tender, about 8 minutes.

2. Add the broccoli and soy sauce and cook until the broccoli turns bright green, about 5 minutes.

3. Add the celery, bok choy, mushrooms, almonds, and red wine and stir well.

4. Lower the heat to medium-low, cover the pan, and cook until the veggies are tender, about 5 minutes.

5. Spoon the rice into individual bowls and top with the stir-fried beef and vegetables. Serve with additional soy sauce on the side.

Tofu and King Oyster Asparagus Stir-fry

Serves 4 ✎ Prep time: 15 minutes ✎ Cook time: 25 minutes

VEGAN / VEGETARIAN

King oyster mushrooms have a different cap-to-stem ratio than other oyster mushrooms, which make them stand up well in a stir-fry. Here, they are combined with asparagus and tofu, excellent complements to the heartiness of the mushroom. This recipe will be ready fast, so have your ingredients prepped!

2 teaspoons sesame oil

1 (1-inch) piece ginger, minced

2 garlic cloves, minced

½ yellow onion, diced

2 tablespoons soy sauce

1 bunch fresh asparagus, cut into 1-inch pieces

1 can water chestnuts, drained

1 (16-ounce) package extra-firm tofu, drained

1 cup corn kernels, fresh or frozen

½ to 1 pound king oyster mushrooms

1 bunch bok choy, chopped

2 cups sui choy, chopped

Cooked white rice, hot

1. In a large skillet or wok, heat the sesame oil over medium-high heat.

2. Add the ginger, garlic, onion, and soy sauce, and cook until the flavors begin to meld and the onion looks translucent, about 6 minutes.

3. Add the asparagus and water chestnuts and cook, stirring constantly, until the asparagus is bright green but still firm, 2 to 3 minutes.

4. Add the tofu, corn, and mushrooms and cook, stirring frequently, until the tofu browns on one side, 2 to 5 minutes.

5. Add the bok choy and sui choy and cook until they are just wilted and tender, 2 to 4 minutes.

6. Serve hot over cooked white rice.

Pink Oyster Mushroom Fried Rice

Serves 4 🍃 Prep time: 30 minutes 🍃 Cook time: 30 minutes

VEGAN / VEGETARIAN

This recipe is designed to highlight the light pink tonality of this variety of oyster mushroom, but you can use any type of oyster mushroom you have on hand. For the best results when making this dish, use leftover chilled rice from the previous day.

1 teaspoon plus 2 tablespoons sesame oil, plus more if needed, divided

1 medium yellow onion, finely chopped

2 teaspoons minced garlic

1 (1-inch) piece fresh ginger, minced

2 tablespoons coconut oil or butter, salted

4 cups cold cooked rice

½ cup slivered almonds

1½ to 2 cups sliced pink oyster mushrooms

1 cup frozen peas

3 scallions, thinly sliced

¼ cup gluten-free tamari or soy sauce

Freshly ground black pepper

1. In a skillet, heat 1 teaspoon of sesame oil over medium-high heat. Add the onions, garlic, and ginger and cook until the onion is softened, about 4 minutes. Add the coconut oil and the remaining 2 tablespoons of sesame oil.

2. Add the rice, almonds, and mushrooms and cook, stirring constantly, until the mushrooms are tender and the rice is heated through. Add more oil if the rice begins to stick.

3. Add the peas, scallions, tamari, and season with the black pepper. Cook, stirring frequently, until just warmed through and the scallions and peas turn bright green, about 3 minutes.

4. Serve hot.

Tips: Toasted coconut, sesame seeds, or sunflower seeds all make flavorful additions to this dish. Use chopped fresh parsley or chopped celery as a garnish.

Lion's Mane Mushroom Omelet with Bacon

Serves 2 ✺ Prep time: 15 minutes ✺ Cook time: 10 minutes

NUT-FREE / GLUTEN-FREE

If you love bacon and eggs for breakfast, this easy omelet is for you. The hearty, earthy flavor of the lion's mane mushroom nicely balances the rich cheese and bacon with the bright tomatoes. The mushrooms also bring a lovely texture and fullness, making this the perfect omelet to start your day.

4 bacon slices, for garnish
4 large eggs
1 tablespoon milk
1 tomato, diced

¼ cup shredded
   cheddar cheese
⅓ cup shredded lion's
   mane mushrooms

1 teaspoon sliced scallion,
   plus more for garnish,
   if desired
2 slices toast (optional)

1. Line a plate with paper towels.

2. In a skillet over medium heat, fry the bacon until crisp, about 10 minutes. Transfer to the prepared plate and set aside.

3. Pour off most of the bacon grease and save for another use.

4. In a bowl, whisk together the eggs and milk. Pour the mixture into the still-hot frying pan set over medium heat and cook. As the egg mixture is bubbling, sprinkle the tomatoes, cheese, mushrooms, and scallions over half the pan.

5. Cook until the egg is looking solidified on the open side, about 3 minutes. Using a spatula, flip the empty half over the vegetables and cheese.

6. Cook through, turning down the heat if needed to prevent burning, 1 to 2 more minutes.

7. Cut the omelet in half and place on individual plates. Garnish with the bacon on the side and additional scallions sprinkled over the top, if desired.

8. Serve hot with toast on the side (if using).

Tips: Use a large pan to make a thin layer of egg that will cook thoroughly. For a dry but soft omelet, do not use more than four eggs per pan. If you wish to double the recipe, simply prepare double the diced and chopped ingredients and plan to make multiple omelets in batches.

Shakshuka with Gold Oyster Mushrooms

Serves 4 ◈ Prep time: 10 minutes ◈ Cook time: 25 minutes

NUT-FREE / VEGETARIAN

Shakshuka is a traditional Middle Eastern dish, most often served at breakfast but also frequently enjoyed at lunch and dinner. Whereas traditional shakshuka focuses on the tomato sauce base, this version adds oyster mushrooms for another dimension of color and flavor.

2 tablespoons olive oil

1 large yellow onion, chopped

1 bell pepper, seeded and chopped

3 garlic cloves, minced

2 tablespoons tomato paste

½ teaspoon smoked paprika

1 (28-ounce) can crushed tomatoes

Salt

Freshly ground black pepper

8 large eggs

1½ to 2 cups sliced golden oyster mushrooms

½ cup crumbled feta

Crusty bread or pita, for serving

1. In a large skillet, heat the olive oil over medium heat. Add the onions, bell peppers, and garlic and sauté until the onions become translucent, about 5 minutes.

2. Add the tomato paste, paprika, crushed tomatoes, and season with salt and pepper. Bring to a simmer, and cook until the flavors begin to meld and the sauce is fragrant, about 5 minutes.

3. Make a well near the edge of the pan and crack the first egg into it. Mound up the sauce around the egg a bit to contain the white.

4. Continue making wells for the remaining eggs, staggering their placement around the pan.

5. Arrange the mushrooms on top of the sauce, cover, and cook for 4 minutes.

6. Remove the cover and cook until the egg yolks are semi-firm but still jiggle and the whites are opaque, 2 to 6 minutes.

7. Top with the feta and serve immediately with bread.

Tips: To increase the spice, add some red pepper flakes or a tiny pinch of smoked chili pepper. For more flavor, use fire-roasted canned tomatoes or add a few smoked dried tomatoes.

Portabella Personal Pizzas

Serves 4 ✑ Prep time: 10 minutes ✑ Cook time: 10 minutes

GLUTEN-FREE / NUT-FREE / VEGETARIAN

With the meaty texture of a steak and the fun and tastiness of pizza, this dish is great as a trial for anyone hesitant about eating mushrooms.

2 to 4 large portabella mushrooms

4 tablespoons pizza sauce

1 tablespoon chopped green bell pepper

1 teaspoon finely minced basil

¼ cup shredded cheddar cheese

¼ cup shredded mozzarella cheese

1. Preheat the oven broiler to 500°F. Line a large baking sheet with parchment paper or aluminum foil.

2. Wash the mushrooms and remove the stems. Remove the mushroom gills and trim off any damaged areas of the mushrooms, or any dirt that cannot be washed away with water.

3. Place the mushrooms gill-side up on the prepared baking sheet.

4. Place 1 tablespoon of pizza sauce in each mushroom and spread it around.

5. Sprinkle each mushroom cap with the bell peppers and basil.

6. Top each mushroom with the cheddar and mozzarella cheeses, making sure the cheese completely covers the mushroom cap.

7. Broil for 8 minutes, or until the cheese is melted and bubbly. Extra-large mushroom caps may require 1 to 2 additional minutes.

8. Let stand for 2 to 3 minutes before serving.

Tips: The pizzas freeze well. Simply assemble as instructed, wrap in plastic wrap, and freeze. To cook, place the frozen mushrooms on a baking sheet and broil as instructed in the recipe.

Dullexes Dolmas

Serves 6 ✧ Prep time: 1 hour ✧ Cook time: 1½ hours

GLUTEN-FREE / NUT-FREE / VEGETARIAN

Make this unique twist on a traditional Mediterranean favorite with whatever mushrooms you have on hand. Garnish with tomatoes or additional leaves of basil and mint, and serve with a cucumber salad for a refreshing, delicious summer dinner.

1½ pounds fresh or frozen mushrooms, diced

1 medium red onion, diced

1 sprig fresh rosemary, leaves minced

2 tablespoons minced fresh basil

2 tablespoons minced fresh mint

2 tablespoons butter, salted

Salt

Freshly ground black pepper

1 cup rice

3½ cups water, divided

1 (16-ounce) jar grape leaves in brine

2 tablespoons olive oil

Juice of 1 lemon

1. Preheat the oven to 350°F.

2. In a large bowl, mix together the mushrooms, onions, rosemary, basil, and mint.

3. In a large skillet, melt the butter over medium-high heat. Add the mushroom mixture and cook, stirring frequently, until the liquid has evaporated, 10 to 15 minutes.

4. Add salt and pepper, to taste. Set aside to cool.

5. In a medium saucepan, combine the rice and 2 cups of the water and soak for 20 to 25 minutes. Drain and rinse well.

6. Add the soaked rice to the mushroom mixture and mix until combined.

7. Carefully rinse the grape leaves to remove the brine. Remove any stems.

8. Spread out a grape leaf and place 1 tablespoon of the rice and mushroom mixture into the center. Roll the grape leaf like a spring roll or burrito, stopping halfway, folding in the sides, then rolling up the remainder.

continues

Dullexes Dolmas *continued*

9. Place the filled grape leaves, seam-side down, in an 8-by-11-inch baking dish.

10. Drizzle the dolmas with the olive oil and lemon juice. Pour the remaining 1½ cups of water into the baking pan. The stuffed grape leaves should be 90 percent covered with water, but not floating.

11. Cover the pan with aluminum foil to hold in the steam and help the rice cook, and bake for 30 to 45 minutes, until the rice is cooked through.

Tip: Roll the leaves firmly, but not too tightly because the rice will expand when cooking.

Three-Bean Chili with Ground Mushrooms

Serves 8 ✦ Prep time: 30 minutes ✦ Cook time: 3 hours

GLUTEN-FREE / NUT-FREE / VEGAN / VEGETARIAN

This chili is simple to make with a focus on ground mushrooms and beans, resulting in a hearty and full-bodied vegetarian dish. Customize the spiciness to your preference level by increasing or decreasing the amount of jalapeño. This chili also cooks well in a slow cooker or pressure cooker.

FOR THE CHILI

1 tablespoon olive oil

1 medium yellow onion, diced

5 garlic cloves, minced

1 tablespoon dried basil

1 tablespoon dried oregano

1 (15.5-ounce) can red kidney beans, drained and rinsed

1 (15.5-ounce) can black beans, drained and rinsed

1 (15.5-ounce) can chickpeas, drained and rinsed

1 (28-ounce) can crushed tomatoes

2 cups ground frozen mushrooms, thawed

1 small jalapeño pepper, minced

1 teaspoon smoked paprika

½ cup salsa plus more for serving (optional)

FOR THE OPTIONAL TOPPINGS

½ cup sour cream

Shredded cheddar cheese

Bread or crusty rolls

TO MAKE THE CHILI

1. In a large pot, heat the oil over medium-high heat. Add the onions, garlic, basil, and oregano and sauté until the onion is translucent, about 6 minutes.

2. Add the kidney beans, black beans, chickpeas, and tomatoes and stir well. Add the mushrooms, jalapeño, and smoked paprika and stir well.

continues

3. Bring the chili to a boil, lower the heat to medium-low, and gently simmer until the flavors meld and the beans are soft, up to 4 hours.

4. Mix in the salsa (if using) to amp up the spiciness, if desired.

TO SERVE

5. Spoon the chili into bowls and top with dollops of sour cream and a sprinkle of cheese (if using). Serve with bread on the side and additional salsa, if desired.

Tips: The ingredients can be mixed up, stored in an airtight container, and frozen for up to six months. If you like meat in your chili, add 1 pound of ground beef at the sautéing stage. If you are vegan, use a vegan alternative for the the sour cream and cheese toppings, if desired.

Tri-Mushroom Curry

Serves 4 ✒ Prep time: 1 hour ✒ Cook time: 30 minutes

GLUTEN-FREE / NUT-FREE / VEGAN

Rinse and soak the mushrooms the night before, or in the morning before you leave for work, and you'll be able to whip up this curry in no time when you get home. The rice can be cooked while preparing the curry sauce so that both are ready at the same time.

1 cup dried shiitake mushrooms

1 cup dried wine cap mushrooms

2 cups chopped fresh button mushrooms

2 teaspoons coconut oil

½ teaspoon ground cumin

2 teaspoons ground turmeric

1 (1-inch) piece of ginger, minced

2 garlic cloves, minced

1 (13.5-ounce) can coconut milk

¼ cup raisins

1 cup rice, uncooked

2 cups water

Parsley sprigs, for garnish

1. Rinse the shiitake and wine cap mushrooms thoroughly. In a bowl, cover the mushrooms with water and allow them to soak for at least 6 and up to 12 hours.

2. Drain the mushrooms. They should now be reconstituted.

3. In a large saucepan, mix the shiitake, wine cap, button mushrooms, coconut oil, cumin, turmeric, ginger, and garlic and cook over medium-high heat until the mushrooms are wilted, about 8 minutes.

4. Add the coconut milk and raisins, mix until combined, bring to a low simmer, and cook until the flavors meld, 10 to 15 minutes.

5. While the curry is cooking, combine the rice and water in a small saucepan and bring to a rolling boil over high heat.

6. Lower the heat to medium-low, cover, and simmer until the rice has absorbed the water and is tender, 15 to 20 minutes. Using a fork, fluff the rice.

7. Spoon the rice into individual bowls and top with the curry. Garnish with parsley sprigs and serve.

Salmon with Reishi Mushroom–Infused Lemon Sauce

Serves 4 ✐ Prep time: 20 minutes, plus 1 hour to marinate ✐ Cook time: 45 minutes

GLUTEN-FREE / NUT-FREE

This recipe is best with fresh, wild-caught salmon, but frozen or a whole fresh salmon works, too. If using a whole salmon, double the sauce ingredients, cover, and bake the fish in the oven, rather than on the stove (see tip).

8 (1-inch) pieces dried reishi mushrooms

¼ cup dry white wine

4 tablespoons (½ stick) butter

Zest of 2 lemons

1½ pounds salmon fillets

Juice of 2 lemons

Salt

Freshly ground black pepper

Chopped fresh parsley

Fried Oyster Mushrooms in Butter (page 107, optional)

Cooked rice (optional)

1. In a bowl, combine the dried reishi mushrooms and white wine and let sit for 1 hour.

2. In a skillet, heat the butter over medium-high heat until it begins to sizzle.

3. Add most of the lemon zest and salmon fillets and sear on both sides until browned, about 4 minutes per side.

4. Add the mushroom mixture and lemon juice to the pan, cover, and cook until the salmon is cooked through, 10 to 15 minutes. Add salt and pepper, to taste.

5. Remove the mushroom pieces and garnish with the parsley before serving with a side of the fried oyster mushrooms and cooked rice (if using).

Tips: Make sure to have all the ingredients ready to go before starting to cook the salmon, as it will cook quickly once started. To oven-cook the salmon, place the salmon fillets in a large baking dish. Blend the sauce ingredients, including the wine and reishi mushrooms, and pour them over the salmon. Cover the baking dish with aluminum foil and bake in a 375°F oven for about 30 minutes or until the salmon is cooked through.

Grilled Wine Cap Mushroom Kebabs

Serves 4 *⌇* Prep time: 1 hour *⌇* Cook time: 15 minutes

GLUTEN-FREE / NUT-FREE / VEGAN

Try serving these kebabs with hot pita bread and tzatziki, a yogurt and cucumber sauce, for a Mediterreanean-style kebab night.

12 to 18 fresh wine cap mushrooms

12 to 18 button mushrooms

5 fresh rosemary sprigs

2 to 3 tablespoons olive oil

2 large red onions, peeled and quartered

2 red bell peppers, seeded and cut into large slices

2 green bell peppers, seeded and cut into large slices

1 pound medium-to-large cherry tomatoes

Salt

Freshly ground black pepper

1. Preheat a grill.

2. Brush off and rinse the wine cap mushrooms and button mushrooms.

3. In a small glass jar, mix the rosemary and olive oil.

4. Place the jar in a larger bowl and pour hot water around the jar. Let sit for about 7 minutes. Pour out the water and refill with more hot water and let sit for another 8 minutes, until the oil is infused with the rosemary flavor.

5. Thread the onions, red peppers, green peppers, and cherry tomatoes onto the skewers, alternating the onions, peppers, tomatoes, and mushrooms until the skewers are filled.

6. Brush the skewers with the rosemary-infused olive oil and season lightly with salt and pepper.

7. Grill until the peppers are tender and the onions are starting to become translucent, 3 to 6 minutes.

8. Serve hot.

Double Baked Potato with Oyster Mushrooms

Serves 6 ✍ Prep time: 1 hour ✍ Cook time: 2 hours

GLUTEN-FREE / NUT-FREE

Enjoy the richness of baked potatoes with the double deliciousness of extra cheese, sour cream, and oyster mushrooms. Use real bacon, if desired, or substitute with imitation bacon bits for a more vegetarian-friendly option.

6 large yellow or russet potatoes, scrubbed clean

1 tablespoon olive oil

12 tablespoons (1½ sticks) butter, softened, divided

½ cup milk

1½ cups shredded cheddar cheese, divided

3 scallions, thinly sliced, divided

4 cooked bacon slices, crumbled or ¼ cup bacon bits

3 cups chopped oyster mushrooms

1. Preheat the oven to 400°F.

2. Pierce the potatoes multiple times with a fork, rub with olive oil, and wrap them individually in aluminum foil.

3. Bake the potatoes for 1 hour, or until soft. Let them cool until you can handle them, about 15 minutes.

4. Cut off the top one-third of each potato and scoop out the insides, being careful not to pierce the skin.

5. Put the potato insides in a large bowl. Reserve the potato tops and their respective skins.

6. Add 8 tablespoons (1 stick) of the butter, the milk, 1 cup of cheddar cheese, ⅔ of the scallions, and the bacon to the potato insides and stir until combined.

7. Spoon the mixture equally into the potato skins.

8. Sprinkle the remaining ½ cup of the cheddar cheese over each potato and top with the potato cap.

9. Place the potatoes on a baking sheet and bake for 15 minutes, or until the outsides are crisp and the cheese is melted.

10. While the stuffed potatoes are baking, in a large skillet, melt the remaining 4 tablespoons (½ stick) of butter over medium-high heat. Add the oyster mushrooms and cook, stirring frequently, until the mushrooms are dark and wilted.

11. Top each potato with the mushrooms and serve hot.

Tips: You can prepare the potatoes ahead of time, up to just before the second baking. Cover with plastic wrap, and refrigerate for up to three hours. When ready to serve, follow the recipe as instructed. To reheat, bake in a 400°F oven until heated through.

Stroganoff with Beef and Oyster Mushrooms

Serves 6 ✍ Prep time: 30 minutes ✍ Cook time: 1 hour

NUT-FREE

This dish is lighter than classic beef stroganoff, with higher fiber and protein content thanks to the use of mushrooms as a meat extender.

1 pound ground beef

1 medium yellow onion, chopped

3 garlic cloves, minced

½ teaspoon dried oregano

½ teaspoon dried basil

8 ounces ground frozen oyster mushrooms, thawed

2 cups Lion's Mane Cream of Mushroom Soup (page 106)

8 ounces pasta of choice

2 cups frozen peas

1 cup frozen corn

Salt

Freshly ground black pepper

1. In a skillet over medium-high heat, add the ground beef and cook, breaking up the meat with a spoon, until it starts to brown. Add the onions and garlic and cook, stirring frequently, until the onion is translucent, about 4 minutes.

2. Add the oregano and basil and cook, stirring frequently, until the beef is fully browned, 5 to 7 minutes.

3. Add the mushrooms and stir until combined. Add the cream of mushroom soup and stir until combined.

4. Lower the heat to medium-low and simmer for 10 minutes.

5. Fill a large saucepan three quarters full with water and bring to a boil over high heat. Add the noodles and cook according to the package instructions.

6. When the noodles are almost done, add the peas and corn to the beef mixture and stir until combined.

7. Drain the noodles and add them to the beef mixture. Toss until combined, and add salt and pepper, to taste. Serve hot.

Slow Cooker Chicken Dinner with Dried Shiitakes

Serves 8 ✒ Prep time: 15 minutes ✒ Cook time: 5 hours

GLUTEN-FREE / NUT-FREE

Enjoy the warm comfort of an effortless chicken dinner—a great option for family gatherings. I like to set up and schedule the slow cooker in the morning, so that when I get home after a long day, a hot and satisfying dinner is waiting.

1 whole frying or stewing chicken, thawed if frozen

1 large onion, chopped

5 celery stalks with leaves, chopped

5 fresh parsley sprigs, chopped

1 cup sliced dried shiitake mushrooms, rinsed clean

1 tablespoon apple cider vinegar

1 teaspoon salt

½ teaspoon freshly ground black pepper

2 quarts water

1. Add the chicken, onions, celery, and parsley to a slow cooker.

2. Add the shiitake mushrooms, apple cider vinegar, salt, black pepper, and water, making sure the mushrooms are submerged in the liquid.

3. Cover and set the slow cooker for 4 hours.

4. Check the chicken for doneness. If it's starting to fall off the bones, remove it from the slow cooker and strip the meat from the bones. If it's not falling off the bones, cover the slow cooker and continue to cook for another hour.

5. To serve, place pieces of chicken on individual plates and spoon the mushroom mixture alongside.

6. Strain the cooking liquid to use as chicken broth at another time. The broth can be stored in an airtight container in the refrigerator for up to one week or frozen for up to four months.

Pressure Cooker Barbecue Roast with Dried Shiitake Mushrooms

Serves 8 ✥ Prep time: 15 minutes ✥ Cook time: 1 hour

GLUTEN-FREE / NUT-FREE

Add a mushroom twist to your favorite barbecue roast with this simple pressure cooker method. Serve with your choice of side dishes, like mashed potatoes, roasted carrots, or a big green salad, for an awesome weekend dinner with leftovers, or as a meal for a larger crowd.

2 to 3 pound pork roast or beef roast

½ cup barbecue sauce (any)

1 cup dried shiitake mushrooms, rinsed and soaked for 2 hours (see the tip)

2 cups Reishi Mushroom Broth (page 104)

1. Place the roast in a pressure cooker or Instant Pot and cover with the barbecue sauce.

2. Sprinkle the mushrooms around the roast and pour in the reishi mushroom broth.

3. Pressure cook on high for 45 minutes. Let the pressure release naturally.

4. Cut the roast into thick slices and serve with the mushrooms and sauce.

Tips: After soaking the mushrooms for two hours in water, drain and soak them in ½ cup of red wine for 30 minutes for a little extra flavor. Add the mushrooms and wine to the pressure cooker with the mushroom broth and cook as instructed.

RESOURCES

Books

Arevalo, Willoughby. *DIY Mushroom Cultivation: Growing Mushrooms at Home for Food, Medicine, and Soil.* Gabriola Island, Canada: New Society Publishers, 2019.

Cotter, Tradd. *Organic Mushroom Farming and Mycoremediation: Simple to Advanced and Experimental Techniques for Indoor and Outdoor Cultivation.* White River Junction, VT: Chelsea Green Publishing, 2014.

Stamets, Paul, and J. S. Chilton. *The Mushroom Cultivator: A Practical Guide to Growing Mushrooms at Home.* Seattle, WA: Agarikon Press, 1983.

Stamets, Paul. *Mycelium Running: How Mushrooms Can Help Save the World.* Berkeley, CA: Ten Speed Press, 2005.

Trudell, Steve, and Joe Ammirati. *Mushrooms of the Pacific Northwest: Timber Press Field Guide.* Portland, OR: Timber Press, 2009.

Winkler, Daniel. *A Field Guide to Edible Mushrooms of the Pacific Northwest.* Pender Harbour, Canada: Harbour Publishing, 2011.

Websites

The following websites are excellent resources for further reading, and also great places to shop for supplies. Although Amazon does carry some grow-kits from reputable suppliers, I do not recommend ordering grow-kits, plugs, spawn, or syringes from them. Instead, many USA-based suppliers allow direct orders, which helps guarantee quality and viability of your spawn or kits.

Everything Mushrooms: USA supplier, based in Tennessee; carries kits, spore, plug spawn, and more, EverythingMushrooms.com

Field & Forest Products: USA supplier of grow-kits, spawn, and spore syringes, and spawn, FieldForest.net

Forest Origins: USA supplier of grow-kits, spore syringes, and spawn, ForestOrigins.com

GMHP: USA supplier of grow-kits, spore syringes, spawn, and more; this supplier is organic and based in California, Mushroom-Growing.com

Gourmet Mushroom: USA-based supplier of grow-kits, plug spawn, sawdust, and more; has good blog resources as well, GMushrooms.org

Grow Your Pantry: Great site with information guides about specific mushroom varieties, plus cooking and preserving methods, GrowYourPantry.com/blogs/mushroom-guides

Midwest Grow Kits: USA-based supplier of grow-kits, premade substrates, spawn, and spore syringes, MidwestGrowKits.com

Myco Supply: USA-based supplier for everything related to mushroom growing, MycoSupply.com

North Spore: USA-based supplier of grow-kits, spore syringes, spawn, and more; their blog is a very good resource for home growers, NorthSpore.com

Root Mushroom Farm: USA-based supplier of grow-kits, spawn, and spore syringes, RootMushroom.com

INDEX

ABOUT THE AUTHOR

Sarah Dalziel-Kirchhevel lives in rural Canada with her husband and daughter. She is passionate about gardening and finding creative ways to produce food in small spaces. She enjoys empowering others to grow and cook their own food, skills that she believes build confidence. Sarah is the founder of WearingWoad.com and a partner and writer at JoybileeFarm.com.

CPSIA information can be obtained
at www.ICGtesting.com
Printed in the USA
JSHW051155200921
18841JS00001B/2